Legends of Kids TV 2

published in Great Britain by

18 Yeend Close
West Molesey,
Surrey KT8 2NY

www.GJBpublishing.co.uk
@GJBpublishing
#LOKTV2

Illustrations by Garry Vaux
@Garry_Vaux

Back cover montage by
Liquorice Multimedia
facebook.com/liquoricemultimedia

Printed in Great Britain by
www.lulu.com

For Dan & Joe

The Four Wise Men: Puppetry legends (from l-r)
Warrick Brownlow-Pike, Brian Herring, Dave Chapman and Phil Fletcher

CONTENTS

Foreword by Brian Cant............ 1

Introduction............................. 2

Acknowledgements.................. 3

Sophie Aldred.......................... 5

Stanley Bates......................... 10

Geoffrey Bayldon.................... 13

Warrick Brownlow-Pike........... 15

Neil Buchanan....................... 19

Nancy Cartwright.................... 26

Dave Chapman....................... 29

Jonathan Cohen.......................32

Matthew Corbett.....................34

Lee Cornes............................. 37

Dick & Dom............................39

Johnny Edward....................... 41

Simon Farnaby....................... 43

Keith Field.............................. 46

Peter Firmin............................51

Phil Fletcher........................... 55

Keith Harris............................ 63

Brian Herring..........................65

Jeremy Hitchen.......................68

Sarah Jane Honeywell 74

Wayne Jackman...................... 76

Chris Jarvis............................. 83

Paul Kasey..............................86

Pui Fan Lee.............................98

Carol Lee Scott...................... 100

Christopher Lillicrap.............. 102

Maria Morgan........................106

Erkan Mustafa........................112

Hugo Myatt........................... 114

Nigel Plaskitt........................ 116

Lee Pressman........................121

Tony Robinson...................... 124

Michael Rosen.......................125

Sid Sloane.............................127

John Sparkes..........................130

Susan Stranks........................137

Hacker T. Dog.......................142

David Tate.............................146

Brian Trueman.......................148

Tim Whitnall.......................... 156

Nick Wilton...........................159

Henry Woolf 164

Francis Wright....................... 166

In Memoriam........................ 171

FOREWORD

"I'm delighted to add a foreword to Garry Vaux's second book of Legends of Kids TV.

The first one took me back down memory lane where I was able to recall the wonderful programmes I was lucky enough to work on.

My early years as an actor were mostly spent in theatre work and I was only introduced gradually to the quite different world of television: a world growing larger little by little, taking in not only the talents of actors but writers, musicians, singers, teachers, artists, comedians, directors, producers and technicians.

I was privileged to work with some of the best of these, many of whom feature on these pages.

They were joyous years and I thank Garry for compiling such a wonderful collection of memories and in so doing supporting the work of Great Ormond Street."

Brian Cant

Brian is known and loved for the his work on Play School, Playaway, Trumpton, Chigley, Camberwick Green, Bric-a-Brac and Dappledown Farm. He is also proud to be involved for many years with work for The Variety Club of Great Britain and Children With Cancer, amongst others, both of which support Great Ormond Street. Brian was voted the best loved children's television voice in 2007 and is also a recipient of a Children's Television Special Award from BAFTA in 2010.

Thank You

Jack Haywood

Martin Cross

Waen Shepherd

Jenny at secondskinagency.com

Sarah Orton at wacpr.com

Jonjo Batbags cob-web weaver at Grotbags.net

George Littell

Kevin Littell

Rick Jones

Peter Dougan

Lisa Marie

Lisa at Spin Publicity

and everyone else who has helped in the
production of this book along the way

Photo credits unknown except: front matter page Phil Fletcher, p12. Lisa Marie, p17 & 18, Warrick Brownlow-Pike, p20, 23, 24 Neil Buchanan, p28 Nancy Cartwright p30 Steve Ullathorne p32 & 33 Jonathan Cohen p38 Lee Cornes p41 & 42 Johnny Edward p55, 58, 59, 61 Phil Fletcher p64 Keith Harris p66 Brian Herring p72 Garry Vaux p74 & 75 Sarah Jane Honeywell p 78 & 81 Wayne Jackman p84 Chris Jarvis & Pui Fan Lee p101 Carol Lee Scott p104 Christopher Lillicrap p120 Garry Vaux p122 Lee Pressman p124 Tony Robinson p126 Seven Stories p128 Sid Sloane p31 John Sparkes p154 Brian Trueman p156 Henry Woolf p161, 162, 165 Nick Wilton p167, 169, 170 Francis Wright.

# INTRODUCTION

Welcome to this second instalment of legends of Kids TV. It's packed to the brim with interviews, chats and Q&As with 44 stars covering over 50 years of children's television.

Television and radio are a vital cog in any child's upbringing and, done well, it can stay with us well into adult life. It fires the imagination at an early age and can inspire us to achieve great things. Some of the people in this book have already done it moved onto other things and some are making a name for themselves right now.

Everyone will have their own personal legends depending on the programmes you watched, but this selection covers nearly 150 different shows and includes presenters, performers, musicians, writers, entertainers, voice artistes, puppeteers, physical performers, storytellers and comedians.

There were a few people I found difficult to track down initially, but I found that with a bit perseverance you can get your rewards, so this book is definitely a testament to not giving up! I'm also pleased to have a couple of reunions in the pages of this book. Firstly, Maria Morgan and Keith Field from 'A Handful of Songs' as well as Grotbags and Croc from Rod Hull's 'Pink Windmill Show'.

I can guarantee you explosions, monsters, animals, royalty, West End stars, award winners, cartoons, stupid deaths, time-travelling tales, bogies, aliens, funny stories and puppets galore as well as plenty of iconic faces which I hope will have those memories flooding back. So, hop aboard the nostalgia train and have your tickets ready...

Garry Vaux

@Garry_Vaux
#LOKTV2

SOPHIE ALDRED

DOCTOR WHO, CORNERS, ZZZAP!, WORDS AND PICTURES, DENNIS
AND GNASHER, MELVIN & MAUREEN'S MUSIC-A-GRAMS, TREE FUM TOM

I think it's fair to say that Sophie has had a varied career in children's television. From on-screen presenting to TARDIS travels and dalek bashing to learning magic and voicing one of the most iconic male comic characters. It's also a tale of fun, laughter and lifelong friendship.

My mum was reminding me just the other day that I owe my audio career to my brother. When he was young she said he was too lazy to read so I used to read to him a lot and I used to just love doing the voices and the characters. We also used to have a record of Johnny Morris reading all the 'Thomas the Tank Engine' books and he just had the most brilliant way of interpreting a narrative and we was just a master of voices as well and really brought them to life. He was fantastic on 'Animal Magic' when he used to narrate wildlife films and give all the animals voices, he got them spot on, so I learnt from him. He was excellent.

In those days listening was more of a medium than maybe it is today, now we're very into viewing, but there wasn't as much telly geared up for kids, so I used to listen to things such as 'Listen with Mother' and when I was a bit older my brother, a friend and I used to pretend we were a radio station as I'm sure loads of kids still do. We were 'Radio 25 – Kidbrook Grove – Listen in now!' and we would do all these weather reports and record them on a very state of the art cassette player that my dad had got from work, so that was another bit of voice stuff and here I am now making a living out of silly voices.

I went straight from school to Manchester University and did a drama degree which was great. It was quite academic but we got loads of opportunities to perform and I was there with some really interesting people including Simon Hickson (of Trev & Simon fame) who started doing their 'swing your pants' characters while I was there and people like Doon Mackichen who's a good friend of mine, plus different types of people I'd never met before who went on to do different types of things in design, lighting and sound etc, but we got a lot of opportunities to perform there and I took them all. I did a lot of Edinburgh Fringe, and if there was a play I would want to be in it. I graduated from Manchester and realisd that you needed to have an Equity card to work, so that was my next goal. But you couldn't get an Equity card without working and you couldn't work without having an Equity card, so that was quite an interesting little conundrum, but I finally got round that by persuading a friend to be in a singing duo with me in Working Mens Clubs and we got in on our variety ticket.

That was an education! I didn't open my mouth because I come from Blackheath and sounded very posh, and Paul, who I was with, is a Mancunian, so that was ok, so he did all the talking and I just shut up and sang when it came to my turn. We used to do Everley Brothers numbers and we dressed up in the part, I had a 1950s strap dress and he had the full teddy boy outfit. It was good fun but hard work, though.

After I'd graduated I'd always hoped to be a 'Blue Peter' girl, which was my big aim but I ended up being a 'Doctor Who' girl, so that's not bad! I was always quite confident that I would do what I wanted to do and always had a plan. I was quite a good business person and knew what steps I'd have to take, ie getting an Equity card, then getting an agent and then just working as much as possible.

The first TV job I got was 'Doctor Who' but almost immediately after that I got the job presenting 'Corners' as well, so I recorded 'Doctor Who' first, but that needed time to be edited and 'Corners' was actually transmitted first, in which I presented a piece with Keff McCulloch who had composed Sylvester's Doctor Who theme tune so they thought it would be really funny if I went to cover it. I remember that day vividly, going to his studio and pretending not to know anything about it!

It was funny when I saw the very first bit of script I had to do in the read through for the audition for Ace, something just sort of clicked and I knew how to play her. She's not like me at all, I come from Blackheath, I had a very happy childhood and a very good upbringing and went to a very good school and Ace didn't, but there was something about her that resonated with me, I don't know what it was really but I just knew I knew how to play her. She was a tomboy, a feminist, strong but vulnerable, easily hurt and could have her heart broken – that all sort of resonated with me and although the facts of our life were different there was something emotionally about her that I really understood.

"I felt like I could run forever, like I could smell the wind and feel the grass under my feet, and just run forever." Ace

Sylvester is GREAT. We're really good mates. He taught me such a lot. He taught me to ask questions and not just follow the script, check that things made sense and were going to work and we just had the most tremendous fun, he's got a very big heart and he's an extremely generous person. He's a complete one off, there's no one like Sylvester, his eyebrows alone should be given their own Equity card!

I think Ace would love the Weeping Angels. They've been the real iconic ones of new Who. It's that typical old thing that Who does of taking something every day, be it a shop dummy, and turning it into something really scary.

When I was growing up my own Doctors were Jon Pertwee and Tom Baker. I think if they travelled with Ace Jon Pertwee's Doctor would probably not have known what to do with her but he'd have got very cross with her because she didn't follow the rules and as for Tom's, they would have probably have exploded. They were both larger than life! I suppose Ace might have been like a modern Leela for him, there are similarities between Ace and Leela, although Leela was less dressed and I wouldn't have been able to cope with the cold! I've worked with Tom on other things like children's radio and met him at conventions and get on very well.

After 'Doctor Who' I seemed to be able switch quite easily to other work because people knew me from presenting 'Corners' and they knew me for my singing work as well. It wasn't like I was just doing one particular sort of work. It was a blessing and a curse because the blessing was that I could do anything, and I did just do whatever I was asked to do, but the curse was that producers and directors didn't quite know where to place me, whether I was an actress a presenter or a singer or a musicals person, so that was interesting. I started to get into voice overs eventually after a lot of children's telly. I did a lot for the Media Merchants down in Maidstone with Neil Buchanan. First of all co-presented a programme called 'It's a Mystery' with Neil, then they asked me to do a new character on 'Zzzap!' because they wanted to bring a different character in. I think they'd seen some of the crazy characters that I used to play on the pre-school programming for the Children's Channel, which was filmed down in Maidstone too, so I was very happy to do 'Zzzap!' for them because that was another very different thing. Minnie the Mini Magician was very broad mime really and a comedy character so that was very good, then they asked me to do straight presenting on Saturday mornings talking to pop stars on sofas and things like that, which again is incredibly different. So I've been incredibly lucky to have this variety even in children's TV. Looking back, it's been amazing that people did employ me for a variety of different things.

I was such a huge fan of Dennis the Menace when I was growing up and my brother's still got his collection of old Beanos up in my mum's attic, that was something like 'Doctor Who' that was such an icon really. I went up for the part and tested out for quite a few different characters and didn't hear anything from them so I just assumed I hadn't got the part, but it was while I was out in L.A. at a 'Doctor Who' convention that I got an email from my agent months later saying they've given me the part of Dennis the Menace and I couldn't believe it. It was such good fun as well because the rest of the cast were absolutely brilliant, as they always are in animation and audio. There are some very talented people, because if they weren't talented they wouldn't be getting the

Sophie Aldred

jobs. It was just a real laugh to do. We had a fabulous voice director, an American guy called Frank Gresham, who was really good fun and he was getting his head around the British cultural phenomenon of Dennis and we recorded it in one of my favourite recording studios, the Sound House in West London.

I seem to have had good luck playing boys, what with that and 'Tree Fu Tom' I do for Cbeebies now, which is an absolute dream of a job, working with another fantastic voice director Dave Peacock in another of my favourite studios – The Sound Company. It just felt so wonderful to be playing this iconic character and it was a good feeling.

I work with Tim Whitnall on 'Tree Fu Tom' and I'd heard about Tim because I'd worked with Bob Golding on 'Dennis the Menace' and Rob Rackstraw, Teresa Gallagher and Jo Wyatt who all knew Tim and I kept hearing about this legendary Tim Whitnall and then I met him on 'Tree Fu Tom' and he's just the most amazing guy, he's so versatile and he's also a fantastic writer who's also written a biopic that was screened on BBC4 about Kenny Everett. We also do promos for Disney Jr so we sometimes bump into each other for that too. We got on so well it was really lovely and he's become a mate.

I also worked with David Tennant on 'Tree Fu Tom' as well and it's *just* possible we may have swapped the odd Who story! I'd worked with him once before on a spin-off 'Doctor Who' audio before he was the 10th Doctor for a company called Big Finish, who make fantastic, original 'Doctor Who' stuff using all the actors who used to be in the show and have been flying the flag for 'Doctor Who' since it went off air in 1989 and are now an incredibly successful company who've extended the range to 'The Tomorrow People' and 'Sapphire & Stee'l. This story was called 'Colditz', which as it suggests, has the 7th Doctor and Ace landing in Colditz and trying to get out and he was playing a horrible Nazi commandant and he was a right nasty piece of work. David, himself, was absolutely great. He has a real presence when he walks into a room and it was great to work next to him on 'Tree Fu Tom'. He really gives it 100% and gave such a lot of character to this funny little acorn character he plays.

My own children have seen some of the work I've done and are quite proud, but it must be funny for them because it's sort of what they're used to, they've grown up knowing what I do and they're beginning to do their own things now. Adam, my eldest is in 'Tree Fu Tom', he's the boy at the beginning and the end, and William, who's 9, has just done his first job recently with me on a Disney promo and they both love acting – a chip off the old block.

As for the highlights of my career, I can honestly say I've enjoyed everything I've ever done, right from the seemingly humblest commercial voice over. I really like people and like interacting with people. I think of 'Doctor Who' but then I think of 'Melvin & Maureen's Music-o-grams', rolling around on the floor at the rehearsal rooms laughing my head off at some of the mad things we used to do. Then there's going to Jersey to film 'Words & Pictures' when my little boy was tiny and all the fantastic things I got to do on childrens' telly like fly a plane and going to investigate lots of different things - playing the female lead in 'Lust' a West End musical at the Haymarket opposite Denis Lawson and doing panto in Hull with Les Dennis were other highlights. I've been so lucky to have done such a variety of fascinating and different things I can't really pick one out. Who's got to be up there and one of the best things about working on 'Doctor Who' was meeting and working with Sylvester. We're friends for life.

Sophie Aldred

Dennis the Menace

STANLEY BATES
BUNGLE - RAINBOW

As bears go 'Bungle-bonce' must be as well known as the likes of Rupert, Yogi, Fozzie...and Sooty! Several actors donned the famous bearskin in the Rainbow house but Stanley has, by far, played him the longest, but despite such a long stint in the role, Stanley's career also takes in Shakespeare and a classic vintage horror movie.

I started life as a professional actor at the age of 14. I was at grammar school in Guildford and whenever the local repertory theatre wanted a boy to be in a play the school were very good and let me perform. I also went to the Edinburgh Festival with two plays whilst I was still 14 and regularly appeared at the Guildford Rep. Theatre with a professional company.

I went to drama school when I was 16 and after I left, it was by a fluke that I just happened to be in an agents office up for a part and as I came out I bumped into the person in charge of the Bristol Old Vic. He asked me what I was doing and said that he was just about to cast for the part of the little monkey in Beckett with Paul Eddington and Robert Lang at Bristol, which I jumped at and I played that role at the Bristol Old Vic for 6 years. I've been in lots of classical pieces too. I did a 16 country tour with the Bristol Old Vic for Shakespeare's quartercentenary playing the boy in 'Henry V' and Moth in 'Love Labour's Lost'. After leaving the Bristol Old Vic I worked in various repertory theatres throughout the country; the Actor's Company with Ian McKellern, the Cambridge Theatre Company, the Royal Court, I also played Mrs Dale's grandson in 'Mrs Dale's Diary' for the BBC, did quite a lot of BBC radio plays and worked for Roman Polanski in one of his early films called 'The Dance of the Vampires'. I then did another horror film 'Theatre of Blood' which has become an iconic film now.

I did various television work for the BBC and ITV including 'Play for Today', then I was asked to go and see Pamela Lonsdale, who was the 'Rainbow' producer at the time and she asked me if I wanted to play Bungle, so I thought, why not – let's have a go. They had done one series of 'Rainbow' before I joined with John Leeson playing Bungle and David Cook as the presenter. I'm not sure how many years I did it for, slightly less than Geoffrey, but I appeared in over 900 episodes in total.

After quite a number of years I was asked if would like to write for 'Rainbow', which I did and I really enjoyed the writing very very much. Even though I'd stopped playing Bungle then, I carried on writing for it until it came to an end. I also wrote some other children's things for Thames television but overall I spent more time Bungling for 'Rainbow' than I did writing for it.

When I started to play Bungle I didn't think for one moment I'd be playing him for so long. Like all those things, you go into a series never knowing how long it will run for. It might have only done one series then finished, but after every contract, none of us knew immediately whether we'd be re-contracted or the series would be continuing, but in the end it became very successful and built each year upon it's success.

It does get extremely hot wearing a bear suit, especially in a studio under a lot of very powerful lights but being hidden in a suit does give you a certain amount of leeway to be a lot more outrageous than you would be if you were being yourself, you can get away with a lot more. It's not comfortable, but it can be fun!

Rehearsals were quite outrageous at times, there was innuendo in everything, but it wasn't ever written into the scripts. I suppose you can find innuendo in most things, but we had a schools adviser who would go through all the scripts and edit them, so it would change if they didn't approve. We just used to lark around in the studio and had fun. We laughed a lot, we laughed a great deal and that was one reason I carried on playing Bungle for so long. It was quite hard work because we did 3 shows a week, we'd start reading and rehearsing 3 shows on a Friday, rehearsed on the Monday and the Tuesday and we were in the studio on Wednesday and Thursday and back with the next 3 shows on the Friday and we were doing that for 3-4 months, so it was quite hard work really. It was much harder work for the musicians because they had to compose all their music as well.

"...and then Rod & Roger could get their instruments out and Jane's got two lovely maracas!" Bungle (Twangers Video)

I was Bungle in the famous 'Twangers' YouTube video and I'm ashamed to admit that I actually wrote it, but it was never meant for broadcast. Someone did another spoof one which wasn't innuendo, it was just pure filth, I wasn't responsible for that! When I stopped playing Bungle it was interesting to see other people playing that role, but I didn't feel possessive towards the character. It was much easier to sit down and write for the character and not nearly as so hot.

It felt very much like a family. It's like any play you do that has a considerable run, that also develops into a family because you spend 3 or 4 weeks rehearsing with the same people, you then spend 3 months, 6 months, even a year working with the same people so inevitably it becomes a family. Over all that time I don't think there were any real squabbles between the artists, I think everyone got on very well, you just had a job to do so you had to get on a do it.

When 'Rainbow' ended I seem to remember that Thames Television were coming to the end of their license. I don't know why 'Rainbow' was never repeated as other programmes were. I think it would be a great mistake to try and recreate it as it would obviously never be the same but I do think it's a great shame that they don't repeat it. I think it just needs somebody to make the decision to do it, I think.

Stanley as Bungle

I carried on writing, but not for television, I wrote some pantomimes for amateur theatres which I still do occasionally.

The 16 country tour with the Bristol Old Vic was a huge highlight of my career – it was a hugely successful tour and being at the Bristol Old Vic for so long with such illustrious company. 'Theatre of Blood' was just great fun too, but I have to say you couldn't have worked with a nicer person than Vincent Price. He was just one of the nicest guys to work with. Within two days he knew everybody's names whether you were in front of the camera or behind the camera and just made the whole thing a pleasure.

It's great how programmes start as somebody's idea at Thames TV which got built on and expanded and it became the success that 'Rainbow' was. I do still get recognised surprisingly, it does crop up every now and again, but my main memory of 'Rainbow' was that we had a lot of laughs together. We just used to enjoy ourselves.

Stanley Bates

There can't be many actors who turn down an iconic role only to go and create another. Geoffrey could easily have been piloting the TARDIS and galavanting around the universe instead of donning Catweazle's raggedy clothes. The Doctor Who theme continued somewhat when he played The Crow Man opposite 3rd Doctor, Jon Pertwee in Wurzel Gummidge, but what attracted him to the role of Catweazle?

Everything! From the word 'go' it came as something of a great shock. At the time (in the 1970s) everything else on TV was working class, no sentiment and not much comedy and what comedy there was, was loud.

Suddenly, this came along. It was for children but also for adults. My agent said to me 'I've just read the first page. One word – MAGIC' It was funny, not sentimental. What sentiment there was, was underneath.

It was written wonderfully with great charm by Richard Carpenter and if I'd say to Richard that Catweazle wouldn't say something in particular he would just say to me 'Cut it – it's your character.'

Geoffrey as The Crow Man

Catweazle and The Crow Man in 'Wurzel Gummidge' were both magical figures. The Crow Man was more frightening but cares. He cared for Wurzel.

One time Wurzel knocked off The Crow Man's hat and he said 'Alright! That's it! I could destoy you! I could burn you!' and Aunt Sally (at her worst) said 'I've got the matches'.

I've played a lot of old men in the theatre and in Shakespeare and it doesn't really fit on television.

When work came in I said to my agent 'don't tell me if it's an old man!' and one time he asked me 'Would you like to work for 52 weeks?' I was out of work at the time and I said 'Oh my god, give me 10 minutes' but in the end I decided I'd be too old for too long!

As for 'Doctor Who', science fiction doesn't catch my eye and I turned down the part of The Doctor. After they gave it to William Hartnell I began to have second thoughts but 'Catweazle' came along and I made that my own.

I've done lots of different roles including a play with Keith Michell in the last few years where I was jitterbugging like no ones business. I was surprised I could do it!

The most important role I had was the very first one. I played Lord Ogilvy in 'The Clandestine Marriage' at the Old Vic Theatre School. Lord Ogilvy is a wonderful character to play.

The director Wendy Toye came to see it and she thought I was older than I was and gave me my first job in CB Cochran's musical 'Tough at the Top'. I signed up for 6 months but he said 'I'm releasing you as I know you'll be going to Stratford and don't want to stand in your way.'

Catweazle

WARRICK BROWNLOW-PIKE
OUCHO T CACTUS & DODGE T. DOG - CBBC, SPACE PIRATES,
ED & OUCHO'S EXCELLENT INVENTIONS, HACKERTIME, SCOOP

Warrick is the first of several puveyors of the puppeteerial art to feature in this book. Proof, if any is needed, that some men can indeed do more than two things at once! Among his many credits he's best known for bringing CBBC's Oucho and Dodge T. Dog to life and it was apparent to Warrick he knew his calling in life from a very early age...

I knew when I first saw 'The Muppet Show' at the age of around two of three that this is what I wanted to do, and I had blind faith from that moment on. There really wasn't any other option. I always knew it would happen too, I never doubted that I'd be working with puppets. I watched every puppet show that I could, focusing on the work of the Henson company. My parents bought me a video camera and my Mum made me some fantastic puppets, I'd give her a drawing and say 'I want this to be a puppet... and i want his hands to move... and I want him to have lots of facial expressions... and I want it to look really professional... how fast can you make it?!' I'd hook the video camera up to the TV and pretend to be a professional puppeteer. I'd be lip synching to songs and coming up with little sketches for hours. I still have it all on tape!

Jim Henson means alot to me. He was a master puppeteer and a wonderfully creative person. He wouldn't just think about a character, he'd think about the world that character lived in and what might go on in that world, and who else might live there. He was a genius. Everything that happens in my life at this point seems to be traceable back to Jim Henson, he's had an immense impact on my life. I have a career in puppetry because Jim inspired me with his work, and I met my partner whilst working on a puppet TV show and we have a beautiful daughter and a lovely house, and it is all thanks to Jim!

I think that Puppetry can go very far and it can be used to get lots of points and messages across. I mostly stay in the bright and funny world of children's television (and occasionally adult) but there are so many people out there at the moment that are using different of styles puppetry to entertain, engage and educate. And they're doing a wonderful job. I've worked with Phil Fletcher (Hacker T. Dog) on a number of films for children's charities and people really do seem to sit up and listen when a puppet tells them how good something is!

As for as arm fatigue goes my arm rarely hurts. It'll only ever hurt if it's stuck through a hole or something, but most of the time it's just up above my head floating freely. Often the stage manager will have to remind me to put my arm down and rest it. It's a habit to have it in the air, and I just forget that it's up there!

The hardest thing is remembering your lines, watching your monitor, using the arm rods/live hands and moving around on a chez-lounge on wheels type trolley whilst being aware of everyone else and everything else around you ALL AT THE SAME TIME. It's a lot to take in and there's an art to getting it right but after a while it does become second nature. Luckily I get to perform on TV everyday and you can really iron out any issues quite quickly.

It was a great feeling bringing the Broom Cupboard back although we weren't really concentrating on that. We just wanted to make it the best we possibly could. We had lots of fun with Ed and Oucho and eventually moved from the CBBC Office onto two shows 'Ed and Oucho's Excellent Inventions' and our BBC2 Saturday Morning show 'Transmission Impossible with Ed and Oucho'. For 'Inventions' they went out on location all over the UK and made children's dreams come true (after nearly ruining their lives) by making their crazy inventions a reality, and in 'Transmission' the duo took to the skies in a blimp! They intercepted the BBC2 airwaves and took over for an hour and half on both saturdays and sundays for the whole summer of 2009. The blimp in reality was studio H at Pinewood studios, I think that place is the closest thing you can get to feeling like you're on one of those old Hollywood lots.

Oucho

I definitely think that now would be a good time to get kids learning "Cactinian." There was so much fan mail sent in that was written in 'Cactinian' that I think a lot of people are already fluent! It is a "lossoli" language that rolls off of the tongue! Oucho occasionally pops into the CBBC office, but he spends most of his time in Canada living the high life just like a celebrity cactus should. 'Ed and Oucho's Excellent Inventions' still airs regularly on BBC2, CBBC and BBC Kids in Canada.

Dodge is cute which means he can get away with anything. He often gets things wrong, but is always convinced that he's right. He comes up with the most hare-brained schemes and Chris 'Yonko' Johnson daftly listens to him and goes along with it. His outfits are all designer stuff. Dodge will be the first to tell you that he is a very famous dog and has designers sending him clothes all of the time, one of the first things he'd tell you is that he has met and spoken to the Queen. He wore only a collar and purple tie for that occasion!

There are too many funny moments to list. Me and Phil Fletcher (Hacker T. Dog) always have such a laugh when we are working, sometimes I can't breathe for laughing. He often makes me laugh by saying something bizarre during a live link. I once had to be inside an old upright piano so that Oucho could sit on top of it. There was a hole in the top and my arm was straight up through it. Now, pianos are VERY narrow and are not made for a six foot tall man to be inside of, very uncomfortable! It's even worse when there is a six foot tall man stuck inside a piano WITH AN ANGRY WASP! It stung me right on the back and there was nothing I could do about it, everyone thought it was hilarious. I thought it was torture! I've also been left in the middle of a football field stuck in a box in a thunder storm. Everyone ran when the skies opened, they grabbed the puppet and ran... and left me in the box!

I've been lucky enough to work with puppet icons such as Elmo, Fozzie Bear & Gordon T. Gopher. Gordon had a hole in his head, I had to stitch it up before we did the 25th Anniversary of CBBC, but it was a great honor to perform Gordon with Philip Schofield, and he was hilarious with his adlibs! Working with Elmo is always such a pleasure, and when I first worked with him it all clicked together in my head and I said 'Ah, this is how it's done properly!' Kevin Clash is so slick and such a brilliant performer. He also writes/directs and produces Sesame Street! He told me that I was "good and funny" and I nearly fainted!

I met Eric Jacobson who performs Miss Piggy, Fozzie and Animal when we did The Muppets on the 'X Factor'. I was assistant puppeteer for his characters, which means performing anything that the main performer cannot. Mostly arms, sometimes legs and the occasional eye movement. I did get to perform Animal dancing with Miss Piggy to 'Dance With Me Tonight' for a video that plays on the big screens behind Olly Murs on his tour. That was a dream come true! I had an Animal puppet when I was a kid, and now here I was performing the real thing.

Marion & Warrick

I also worked on the adult puppet show 'Mongrels' on BBC3. Marion

Warrick Brownlow-Pike

did get into some odd situations at times. He had to be in the drum of a washing machine, which meant that I had to be under the machine. That was a first! Most of his time was spent inside a tin can dustbin, sadly that wasn't a first. I've performed from inside wheelie bins too. Because we never did the voices live on 'Mongrels' it took so much more concentration than normal. We had to make people believe that these creatures were saying those lines and that they really meant what they were saying.

I do think that there is a market for adult TV Puppetry. 'The Muppet Show' and 'Spitting Image' were major successes, it just takes time for those particular ideas to come back around. Everyone loves puppets (that's what I keep telling myself anyway!) 'Mongrels' series one and two DVDs are on sale and seem to do quite well, so hopefully one day that'll mean that we can do another series?

Designing puppets is something that I also love to do. When you're drawing these characters on the page there is every possibility that they'll be living things within a few weeks and out there for everyone to see. I've designed so many characters and have loved how each one has turned out.

I think meeting the Queen and taking Dodge to 'The Muppets' UK premiere have been my highlights. It's funny because when you have a little celebrity dog on your arm it's like having a pass to go anywhere and meet anyone, take the dog away and I'd just be another weird guy meeting the Queen!

Warrick Brownlow-Pike

Please visit Warrick's website www.brownlow-pike.co.uk

NEIL BUCHANAN
ART ATTACK, FINDERS KEEPERS, IT'S A MYSTERY, NO. 73, ZZZAP!

As a child of the 70s my artistic inspiration was the late great Tony Hart. For the next generation it was undoubtedly Neil Buchanan. These days Neil is still flexing his artistic muscle as well as going back to his musical roots, but what inspired this Master of Modelling, this Professor of Plop Art and this Sage of Splat Attacks? And what is his hope for the future?

My dad really was the greatest inspiration in my life and we were incredibly close. Everything I am today, I owe to him. For an ordinary working man bringing me up in a tough but close community in Liverpool he went against the grain and sat for hours drawing and colouring with me. It was my father that first spotted my talent for drawing and he encouraged me all the way. Of course growing up in Liverpool in the 1960s surrounded by Beatlemania, everybody wanted to be the fifth Beatle and I also spent a lot of time playing in the streets in Aintree dreaming of winning the Cup Final with my heroes Liverpool FC.

Between The Dandy and The Beano it was The Beano every time! Apart from my dad, The Beano was my greatest childhood inspiration... no laughing! I literally lived inside The Beano when I was young. It taught me so much about cartoon drawing and I even used to stick my cartoons on our black and white telly, as the flickering light brought them to life. Walt Disney also made a big impression on me both as a child and later as a 'sort of' grown up on Art Attack... in terms of ideas he was the greatest ideas man ever.

Having enjoyed a brief flirtation with fame and fortune as a rock star in the late-seventies with 'Marseille', our record company collapsed in a morass of litigation and I found myself in a very tight financial corner, what I described as 'the barren years'. During this time, I rented a one bedroom bedsit in Liverpool and lived off cornflakes straight out the packet! I was scanning the local papers to try to find a 'proper job' when I spotted an advert that asked 'Have you ever had breakfast with a gorilla?'

I replied saying "No but I did let a monkey sit on my lap" and sent the photo to prove it of me as a young boy with a monkey. My quirky answer got me through the door for an interview and it turned out the producers of a new anarchic TV show called 'No. 73' were searching for original acts and presenters. I got my first break and was offered a spot on the show as a caricaturist. This gave me a great chance to show the world that I could draw on live TV and by the second series of 'No. 73', I'd blagged my way into a presenting role. I must have done something right because lots of other presenting jobs began to come my way including 'Motormouth', 'Finders Keepers', 'ZZZap!' and 'Animal Crazy'.

As for 'Art Attack', there's quite an amusing story here. There is no room for shy, retiring wallflowers in TV and my agent gave me the best piece of advice ever. He said to me "if you are going to achieve more than 'five minutes of fame' Neil you need to create and develop your own show". After working on the idea with my TV mate Tim Edmunds I went into pitch the concept to the ITV network. But 'Art Attack' was so radically different and 'the suits' in the room initially struggled to see the appeal of an art programme for young people.

With just seconds to go before the end of the 'Art Attack' meeting and my big chance almost gone I spotted a pile of fax paper (back in the dark ages when we all used fax machines!) I asked the panel if I could use some paper and laid it across the boardroom floor in a very long line. Then I borrowed a marker pen and began to draw a long straight line across the paper trail. After several minutes the bemused panel of executives asked "What are you doing?" I replied, "Art... and you've just spent the last two minutes watching me doing it!" 'Art Attack' got the green light from ITV and the rest... as they say is 'Art Attack' history!

I'd like to say my red sweatshirt is beautifully wrapped up in tissue paper and a plastic seal for posterity, but it's probably feeding a family of moths in my very crowded art attic as we speak! The red sweatshirt is still one of the most iconic things about 'Art Attack' people seem to concerned as to the welfare of my 'Art Attic' sweatshirts and 'The Head'!

With six million viewers watching 500 episodes over 17 years I certainly got sack loads of mail and drawings over the years! Even now people Tweet me their art and designs to ask my opinion. My secretary and I tried to respond to as many letters as possible back before the days of social networking, but it was physically impossible to write to everyone. I've always said it's the opinions of my viewers that mattered to me most – in effect each week I had six million art critics watching me!

As we are in Diamond Jubilee year I will share a regal story with you. I'm a huge fan of Her Majesty and think she has done an awesome job being our Queen over

Neil in his Art Attack days

60 years. Winding back about ten years ago I'd been invited to the then owners of 'Art Attack' who had been awarded an international Queen's Award for the overseas success story of TV show's such as mine. I thought it would be fitting to make a castle and nervously waited to speak to the Queen. She looked at the castle long and hard and then asked "What is it made of?" I held my breath, thought of the Tower and replied "Loo rolls ma'am!" Her face lit up with the broadest of smiles and she simply quipped, "Ingenious!"

My favourite piece of work, again, involves Her Majesty. I had the idea to create the Queen's portrait out of a quarter of a million £10 notes, but we wondered where we could get such a vast sum from. After some discussions with The Bank of England, they agreed to loan us the money overnight, as long as we paid the interest!

It was all very dramatic when the security van arrived as we filmed the security guards walking through swirling mist. I was amazed that so much money fitted into nothing bigger than an attaché case! I worked through the night to complete the Big Art and was delighted with the result. The only thing was the cleaner hadn't been told about the project for security reasons and when she came in in the morning and turned on the air conditioning, the whole Big Art nearly blew away!

In terms of my favourite medium, I love acrylic paint, it's easy to work with and dries quickly, but at the end of the day I'm a mixed media man and love to switch from pastels, to crayons, ink pen to paints, as long as I'm being creative I don't mind what I'm working with.

I think people would be amazed just how long and complicated the Big Arts really were. I would spend a good few days working on a new idea and then my team would seek out the props I needed. We would have a full dress rehearsal to get the perspectives right from a bird's eye few and only then begin filming. So although they looked like they were 'thrown' together in a few minutes of fast film, in reality each one took about a week to set up, produce and film.

When I won a BAFTA I remember thinking things like that just don't happen to people like me! Apart from the birth of my two children, it's the most incredible moment of my life... and we won a second one a few years later too!

Funnily enough my show was watched by as many adults as it was children, I don't think the grownups could steal themselves away to cook the tea... especially when I was doing the Big Art. For my younger fans it was all about inspiring young people to 'have a go' that's why my catchphrase was 'Try it yourself!' Somewhere between childhood and the teenage years, young people go from expressing themselves through drawing and painting, to believing that they "can't draw". That's really sad and my main mission was to break down those barriers and hang ups and get a whole generation of young people being creative.

Many of my most loyal Art Attack fans are now in their twenties and thirties and the thing that never ceases to move me is the thanks I receive for being part of their childhood. Loads of people say "Neil, Art Attack was my childhood". The phrases people use the most is "you are a legend" and "you are an inspiration" - I love the fact that every year hundreds of people contact me still to say that because of 'Art Attack' they were inspired to become an artist, an architect, designer, to teach art... that's my greatest legacy and the thing that means the most to me.

Out of all the other shows I enjoyed 'No. 73' the most ... it was riotous, anarchic and live! It taught me so much and was a zany, fun show to be involved in. It gave me a real TV apprenticeship as I was involved with almost every aspect of the show from the writing to performing. It also gave me a great understanding of the technical side of TV as it was a two hour live 'drama' which included guests, comedy sketches, location filming, live bands, animals, you name it - it was all in 'No. 73'.

I think it was probably the most innovative kids' show I have ever seen and as such taught everyone involved with it so much. In fact, it was such good training that so many of the people involved in it went on to do really well in their own careers and many of them are very successful and prominent in the TV industry today.

Going back to my musical roots was a real trip down memory lane and I guess that's why we called the album and tour 'Unfinished Business'. I wrote, recorded and produced the album from my home studio and it was awesome to have an excuse to be back with my oldest friends from my youth in Liverpool and to don the leather jacket and trousers again! The funniest thing was seeing heavy rock fans dressed in Crayola pen costumes when we went on tour – I guess that summed up the two very different sides of career – music and art!

If I had the choice to give up everything I've done on TV to be a heavy metal star instead, I'd say 'absolutely'. Music was my first love and I did give up my chance to go to Liverpool College of Art to be in the band first time around as a teenager. The college principal said I had to choose between art and the music and I never looked back. I appeared on TV in 1977 in the first ever 'Battle of the Bands' and Marseille won! We were signed by Mountain Records and recorded a series of singles and albums and Marseille became the first New Wave of British Heavy Metal (NWOBHM) bands to break into the USA, supporting

Nazareth and Blackfoot in 1980. Sadly, the record company collapsed, and Marseille reluctantly split in the early 1980s until we got together for 'Unfinished Business' in 2010.

There were rumours of my death which all started on Facebook when someone started a page 'RIP Neil Buchanan'. At the time I was on holiday with my family in a remote mountain location in North Wales and I had no idea. My poor elderly mother got the shock of her life, hearing that her son had 'died', as it was several days before we returned to civilisation and a place that had a mobile phone signal. The site received 69,000 condolences in a few days.

The adulation from children I may have inspired and the noise from a heavy metal crowd are so different it would be impossible to say which is a bigger buzz, but I'm not a fan of celebrity or fame for its own sake. I would always rather be remembered and associated for what I do as an artist and musician rather than because I'm simply Neil Buchanan. I find the whole celebrity thing a bit vacuous and think it's much more important for me to focus on developing my talents further and I'm really enjoying the whole thing of establishing myself as a fine artist or 'fine anarchist' as I sometimes call myself these days!

Neil with his BAFTA

By the way, I never did have breakfast with a gorilla, but then I did (as you know) let a monkey sit on my lap and look what happened after that!

As for my favourite artist, I'm a huge fan of the post-impressionist Toulouse Lautrec and both Norman Rockwell and Jack Vettriano have inspired me with their humour, rich narrative and their magnificent artistic ability. I like them all for very different reasons, so would find it very difficult to choose my absolute favourite, but if you pushed me and I was shipped off to a desert island it would probably be one of Toulouse Lautrec's 'greatest hits'.

You'll have to ask the people that have started collecting and buying my original fine art and limited edition prints if my art has got better with age! Funnily enough I started painting 'grown up' pictures because the question I was most frequently asked on Art Attack was "but can you *really* paint?" I guess Neil Buchanan's HOPE STREET and Back Street Games is my response. I'll let my

Neil in his Back Street Games

paintings do the talking. I've always said the greatest honour for an artist is for someone to like your pictures so much that they want to hang them on their walls. So for anyone who does me the honour... thank you!

HOPE STREET came to life out of the dark and sinister rumours on the internet. I started questioning the excesses of modern technology and its negative influences and began to record my own childhood memories in Liverpool in the early 60s long before the days of Facebook, Twitter and the internet, when life seemed simpler. In a series of rough sketches I depicted a time before computers banished us to cyberspace and traffic clogged up our streets... and so the seed of an idea was sown for a new, yet strangely familiar, adventure playground which we've called 'Neil Buchanan's HOPE STREET'.

Whilst I embrace the positive elements of modern technology I hope we never lose site of the magic of the simplicity of childhood. When I went out to play I walked down my very own HOPE STREET everyday with the gift that only children truly possess in abundant measure... imagination. HOPE STREET was a space where you could be whoever you wanted to be, and go wherever you wanted to go, and a place where you could rule the world or win the World Cup and all before tea time.

I want HOPE STREET to take you on a journey. This voyage doesn't involve a long car ride or train trip, because my HOPE STREET is not a place, it's a state of mind... and it's a nice place to be. I'm a sucker for nostalgia and the 12 images capture an evocative snapshot of childhood 'hanging out' in the great outdoor adventure playground, from twisting on the swings and shared bike rides; through fishing with homemade rods, to the arrival of the ice cream man in the street.

But I guess it wasn't going to be long before the cheeky irreverent Scouser in me came to the fore and for 2012 I've created 'Neil Buchanan's Back Street Games'. Everyone has gone Olympics mad this year over the biggest sporting event the country has seen for years, so I thought I would go the opposite way and depict what goes on all over the rest of the country - not just in London. This is the 'smallest' sporting event of the year and features the reality of what really happens in the back streets and parks of little Britain. In many ways you could say these little 'lympics are the real games and the real lasting legacy where young people are inspired to have a go themselves.

If you're anything like me and have thought 'Oh no not another bloomin' souvenir', the Back Street Games is the ultimate antidote to souvenirs! This is 100 per cent not the Olympics! This is smallness on a big scale!

In my 'Athlete's Alley' every event is turned upside down. Wooden crates are transformed into the winning podium, dustbins morph into hurdles, a battered fence changes into the high jump and a bit of old string transforms into the hallowed finishing line. There are five pictures in the collection all with cheeky titles and I've unusually combined a monochrome background, whilst the animated 'Naughty Sporties' are painted in full colour in the foreground.

Neil Buchanan

You can see more of Neils' work at www.neilbuchanan.co.uk

NANCY CARTWRIGHT
BART - THE SIMPSONS, RUGRATS

The Simpsons, voted the Nation's favourite children's TV show in a Channel 4 poll, has been on the air since 1989 and has won a hatful of awards along the way. Nancy is best know as the voice of Bart, but she also lends her vocal skills to Nelson, Ralph, Toddy, Kearney and Database. Nancy won a Primetime Emmy Award for her voice work as Bart, not bad for someone pretending to be a boy all these years!

"I was born in a suburb of Dayton, Ohio called Kettering. Great town. Great folks. Kettering was named after inventor Charles F. Kettering who invented the automatic starter for the car. (Just FYI!)

My first 'public performance' was at the age of 10 with a reading of Rudyard Kipling's "How The Camel Got His Hump" in an all-school competition, for which I received first place. Two years later I was invited to be the youngest member of the Summer Youth Theatre Company, a group of high school students that travels throughout Ohio performing musicals and it was in 1973 when I debuted on stage with The Centerville Town Hall Players in a performance of "Wait Until Dark".

In '77 I created my first character "Lily Padd" who appeared daily throughout the summer on WING radio and following a visit to WING, Warner Bros.' representative, Anne Schwebel, put me in touch with Daws Butler, the voice of Yogi Bear, Huckleberry Hound, Quick Draw McGraw, Snagglepuss and dozens of other characters. It was the start of a 9-year relationship. To many, it would seem a shot in the dark to call a famous artist thousands of miles away to ask for help but I was so young and naïve so I just did what I thought made sense. I had his phone number and I had a phone, so, I called him. Pretty simple. I think sometimes we stop ourselves from ever doing the important things in our life because we are afraid of what "others" might think. Don't worry, take chances. At that time, I had no idea that things would actually unfold the way they did--fortunately for me. The bottom line is, I trusted my muse, and myself--my passion.

Bart's voice was really something that just came naturally to me. I was called to audition for the role of 'Lisa' initially when 'The Simpsons' was a series of animated 'bumpers' for "The Tracey Ullman Show" but as I was looking at the characters and read the description of Bart he seemed much more interesting - "Underachiever and Proud of it!" I asked to audition for Bart instead, gave Matt Groening one voice, and what you hear is what I did! I was hired on the spot.

After approximately 35 short segments run on "The Tracey Ullman Show", Fox TV gave "The Simpsons" its own half-hour TV time slot. The first show aired on January 19, 1990, and the rest, as they say, is history--or in this case: her-story!

We have had over 400 guest stars on "The Simpsons", so it is a little difficult to say who my favorite one is. I love it when a celebrity comes in and is willing to just "play." That is so much fun! Mickey Rooney, Meryl Streep, Anne Hathaway, Zooey Deschanel-- just to name a few. They don't take themselves very seriously and it comes across in their performance; professional but humorous. In fact, it is when they are a bit self-deprecating that I find them most appealing. Some of my other more memorable ones were Michael Jackson, Kirk Douglas, Mel Gibson and Elizabeth Taylor.

As well as Bart I also do the voices of Nelson, Ralph, Kearney, Todd/Rod, Data Base, and Maggie. In addition to "The Simpsons", I've portrayed Chuckie in the cable series "The Rugrats", as well as Rufus the Naked Mole Rat in "Kim Possible" and Todd on Disney's "The Replacements.

After 500 episodes it is not too hard to keep the funniest show on television fresh! I have to pinch myself to remind me that I actually get paid to do all the things most kids get punished for doing: like making burping and farting sounds!

The thing I tell people who ask is that if you want to be a voice over artist you need the ability to make it sound like it is "the first time", in other words, when you are doing a record and the director asks you to "do it again" and "one more time" for about the 10th time, you have to make it sound fresh, as if you have never said it before. Another skill needed is, believe it or not, the ability to "Be a Professional." This is the most basic and a skill anyone from any profession could benefit from. There is a tendency to use the record time to "make friends" or socialize, chat it up, but it's just not the time to do this. You are hired to do a job using your voice; however, it is my professional opinion that during a record, and the time in between, it is best to keep to your work so that the job can be done smoothly and efficiently.

"Is Seymour there? Last name Butz."
Bart

My "tips of success" in the voice-over world extend a little beyond just having a good demo tape (2 minutes in length-maximum) or getting a good agent. I think a few "life tools" are what is needed/wanted.

• Trust your instincts--When that "inner voice" talks to you, listen. In other words, if you get the sense that something is not right, change your mind. Case in point, my audition for the show. Bart vs. Lisa.

• DECIDE exactly what you want to do. And I mean "exactly". Put it in writing. State what you want to do. Obviously you will have to take the steps in order to get whatever that vision is, but without actually stating it, I find it to be a little too ephemeral.

I am at my happiest when I am productive and I am very busy all the time, doing things my agent and my in-house team have gotten as well as things I create for myself by networking. Aside from that, I working on a screenplay, a primetime animated project, an app for the racing world, my non profit work (www.happyhouse.org, www.goodchoicesprogram.org among others) and still have to find time to have a personal life. Still, I do not think I am doing enough! (Hehehe!)

Nancy Cartwright

I had a wonderful mentor but found that as far as mentoring others, I prefer to leave that to the professionals. I taught a class once on "How to Create Characters" but soon realized that it is not my arena. There are plenty of teachers out there who have a genuine skill at teaching. I am not one of them. My own interests actually reach out on a broader scale. Almost 7 years ago, I was selected as the Honorary Mayor of the North Valley, a part of the San Fernando Valley in California that houses about 1.3 million people. This title is not to be confused with an actual "mayor." It is really a PR position, a way to help stay involved in my community. I also love working with a number of child betterment programs such as various Boys and Girls clubs, the Police Activities League Supporters, after school community centers, etc. I feel very privileged that at this point in my career I can actually "pick and choose" what I want to do, and how I want to help. You would have to live under a rock to not notice the illiteracy, the vagrancy, the crime, drugs and lack of personal integrity going on in our neighborhoods. With all the problems we face; I just wanted to do something to help.

I have an e-newsletter, The Nancy News, that keeps people up-to-date on what I have going on. My website, **www.nancycartwright.com**, always has the latest news!"

Nancy Cartwright

DAVE CHAPMAN

OTIS THE AARDVARK, THE SLAMMER, DICK AND DOM IN DA BUNGALOW,
NUZZLE & SCRATCH, HOOPLA, HACKER TIME, ALIENS VS WIZARDS

Dave's career has already seen him in jail, residing in famous single storey accommodation and spending time underneath an aardvark, but he's equally at home on screen or hidden away bringing puppets to life, so I had to ask him the burning question - Creamy muck muck or sloppy ploppy porridge, which do you prefer?

Ah, now...well...there's a question - Literally - Sloppy ploppy porridge is very contained and doesn't get thrown at you as often, and sometimes it's even warm - luxury! However, Dick and Dom in Da Bungalow's signature dish - 'Creamy Muck Muck' was always quite horrendous. We never stooged our reactions to that stuff, and I don't think it ever came out on the show that it was freezing cold. I mean really cold. The show was transmitted through winter and sometimes the many many buckets of muck muck were stored out the back of the Bungalow on the ring road at Television Centre, which meant it was quite a shock when you got your first face-full of the day.

Jim Henson made me go into puppetry. When I was a kid 'The Muppet Show' started and I just went nuts for it, it was so original, so colourful, other worldly, beautifully designed, funny, off-the-wall. It delivered well written, appealing characters again and again. I just loved that show. Jim Henson and all the amazing people who worked with him really smashed it out of the park, for TV puppeteering they changed everything. I see 'The Muppets' influence in every children's TV puppet show that has come out since. Totally unbeknownst to me at the time, my Great Grandmother - Gwendoline Downes, who was Canadian, was an extremely popular live puppeteer on the East Coast of Canada in the 1950's and 60's, so maybe it was always in my blood!

I also used to watch all Johnny Ball's shows as a child - great stuff that was, just one engaging man in a studio giving you mind boggling facts - brilliant. I never missed Saturday morning children's TV, always switched between 'Swap Shop' and 'TISWAS'. I loved a lot of the BBC children's dramas - 'The Box of Delights', 'The Machine Gunners', 'The Phoenix and The Carpet' are ones that stand out. I also enjoyed 'Doctorr Who', and lots of sitcoms - 'Hi di Hi', 'Dad's Army', 'Fawlty Towers', 'Are you Being Served?', 'Sorry', 'Some Mother's Do 'Ave 'em'. I was a huge Frank Spencer fan and my first impersonation was Frank! (Wasn't everybody's?) I did him in 'The Legend of Dick and Dom' a couple of years ago!

I was trained as a puppeteer in 1994 at The Jim Henson Company in Camden, London - now sadly no more, and I auditioned for a Saturday Morning ITV kids show called 'What's Up Doc?' and got the job. Not long after that, I auditioned for the new puppet character on CBBC doing presentation - the links in-between programmes. That turned out to be Otis The Aardvark, which was an absolute blast, and I guess set me up in Children's TV.

Dave Chapman

Otis was great fun, it was in the days when viewing figures were huge, as there wasn't much competition - therefore whenever we shot on location with Otis, everything went a bit crazy - especially if it was school holidays because it seemed that everyone knew who Otis was, and enjoyed his slightly warped view of the world.

I don't know if it's funny, but a kind of weird moment was very early on in my live days at CBBC when a BBC cameraman didn't lock his camera off, and wasn't totally concentrating one afternoon on CBBC. The CBBC studio wasn't built for puppets, so I just used to lie on the floor, or on a puppeteer's dolly (Like a lo-fi skateboard) so I was always lying just underneath frame, and as Otis was talking to camera (Puppeteers all watch monitors, so you can see what you're doing) I noticed the shot start to go south as the camera drifted downwards, but as I was talking in character I couldn't say anything, and it wasn't until my whole head was in frame that they noticed and cut away from me. Must have looked so strange, just some big bloke lying on the floor under Otis, looking at the camera confused.

Working in children's TV is just like working anywhere else! There are good days and tough days. The hours are quite long, sometimes there are lots of lines to learn, sometimes you're on location before the sun's come up - freezing in the middle of nowhere. If you're making a series that takes a few months, it can eat up your life, but generally it's good fun.

Children's TV has changed immensely over the years, mostly for the better, sometimes for the worse! The way children now use media is amazing - TV has to compete with PCs, ipads, playstation, xbox, ds, internet, etc, etc. There are so many alternatives to watching TV that just weren't there twenty years ago. What's encouraging is that children still enjoy a well made TV series and with iplayer and other online viewing services they don't worry about missing an episode, like in the olden days when you had to leggit home after school to get back in time for your favourite show, because if you missed it, it was gone!

I loved playing the series Baddie 'The Beastmaster' in 'The Legend of Dick and Dom' - just great fun to get your teeth into a real wrong 'un. I greatly enjoy making a CBeebies series called 'Nuzzle and Scratch' where I work closely with a brilliant puppeteer called Neil Sterenberg and when we're shooting, we often get delirious, almost to the point of unprofessional, with laugh attacks. Any live TV is real blast as well, though there is less and less of it around. 'Dick and Dom in Da Bungalow' was inspired children's TV that was such a laugh to do, really talented, strong team on camera and off that made this madcap soup of telly that just celebrated being a kid.

"Meet Aubrey. Aubrey here is a sniffer ferret, and believe you me you can't beat a sniffer ferret." - The Beastmaster

Puppeteering is a great job - it is physically demanding, and there's a lot to think about, especially if you're working on live TV. It hasn't changed that much over the years, but when it's done by good performers - it's brilliant.

As for highlights, hmm, that's tricky, there are loads! I drove the Batmobile from 'Batman Returns' round the backlot at Warner Brothers L.A. - that was great, working with The Muppets for the first time was a good gig, working for Ridley Scott on 'Prometheus'. Entertaining the children (and M.P.'s) at the Downing Street Christmas party, For comedy value when we did 'The Saturday Show' in Glasgow in the early 2000's, I once had a company Dinner with Kenny Baker (R2D2) on a Friday night and breakfast with Liam Gallagher on the Saturday morning.. sometimes you do stop and go 'ok, ..now this is weird'.

Dave Chapman

You can visit Dave's own website www.dcblah.com

JONATHAN COHEN
PLAY SCHOOL, PLAYAWAY, MUSIC TIME

A generation of children will have Jonathan to thank for inspiring their interest in music. A frequent face on Play School and Playaway initially, he taught the nation's children about rythms and beats and notes and sounds, without ever being crotchety! It's a musical career that also has seen him arranging and performing in a concert at the Royal Albert Hall for The Queen's Diamond Jubilee.

My love for music started when people noticed that I had perfect pitch aged 4 and my parents bought a piano!

I went on to study at the Royal Academy and after I graduated I was playing in a folk festival at the Albert Hall and John Hosier, head of BBC school's music heard me and invited me to play the piano on 'Making Music'. He then introduced me to Joy Whitby (Play School creator) and she suggested I have a trial as one of the pianists on 'Play School'.

There weren't really any on-screen disasters whilst recording 'Play School' but Julie Stevens narrowly escaped injury when part of a studio lamp blew and showered molten lead onto her foot. It went through one of her boots thank

Jonathan Cohen

goodness! K'too, the cockatoo, was fine with me but once bit Carol Chell! She was not happy. K'too was fine once she (I think it was a she) heard jangle piano music and would then screech and bob up and down. As for the 'Play School' toys, we did string Humpty from a sound boom, and Hamble's head kept falling off. She looked like something from the Exorcist!

After 'Music Time' ended I wrote and MD'd lots of TV shows; 'Melvin and Maureen's Music-a-grams', 'Green Claws', 'Come Outside' (still being shown) and numerous other programmes. I also had time to do more serious work which I was really trained to do. Concerts with various singers etc. I'd started in

I like to listen to all sorts of music but don't listen that much as it's nice to get away from music sometimes! Leonard Bernstein is a hero as he was such a good communicator. Most of the classical greats and Dusty Springfield!

Of my own compositions, my favourites are a piece called "Peace" for choir and orchestra that has been performed at the Albert Hall a few times and "Waverley Rondo" inspired by my passion for the last sea-going paddle steamer in the world....paddle steamer "Waverley".

Every year I present, conduct and play for the Christmas Carol Singalongs at the Royal Albert Hall and around the country. I love it and the audiences have a great time. During this summer we staged a Jubilee Singalong which went down very well.

Jonathan Cohen

I'd say that amongst my proudest achievements was being asked to play for Catherine Bott and James Bowman in concerts around the country, both classical music icons! Also getting children interested in music. It's very humbling to hear people say "if it wasn't for you, I wouldn't be doing music now." Sorry if that sounds conceited, but I was given the chance through television.

Jonathan Cohen

MATTHEW CORBETT
THE SOOTY SHOW, SOOTY AND CO., RAINBOW

"What's that Sooty? Yes, that's right, Matthew's back!" Sooty and Sweep are icons of British culture, a legacy created by Harry Corbett and successfully carried on by his son Matthew and now Richard Cadell. After finding Matthew on Twitter I wanted to find out if he had time for a Q&A, which he did, so in other words, you could say I was thinking "Is he quizzy? Hope he's not busy!"

What was it like working on Rainbow & had it changed much when going back with Sooty? Rainbow was crazy. It was so multicoloured I felt drugged up! Haha. But to be honest, I loved it. All the cast and crew where so.. "down to earth" and I made lots of friends. Although my singing differed (in my opinion). When I joined back to Sooty it felt as if I'd lost a member of the family but Sooty filled that gap up. I missed a lot of the cast and there was such a shock... Singing happy man to Man with his hand up a bears arse!!

Can you put your finger on how your dad managed to make a mute puppet so loveable? No I can't. My Dad was just too.. magical.

Do you think Sooty's magic skills influenced David Nixon in someway? Haha I wish! I love David's work and I'm very proud of him! Sooty's magic is just too secret for anyone else. He has that magic to get millions of children tuned into CITV every morning to watch him and his adventures.

Do you ever find yourself telling children off in a way you have done to Sooty before? Yes!! Often I've had my wife's friends children over who are huge Sooty fans and if one misbehaved I'll say something witty and they'll giggle and say something about how I once said that in a Sooty episode. I just can't help it!

Looking at clips online it seems you did quite a few long scenes in one go, were there lots of rehearsals? As I wrote a lot of the episodes, I was pretty rehearsed myself and would get an episode filmed within 2-4 days. This happened to a lot of children appearing on the show, but as the puppeteers need to have a perfect queue to 'Squeak' Sweep or make Sooty 'move', they would often get payed extra for a scene filmed in one take.

Do you think Sweep's method of speaking inspired the Clangers? That would be a question to ask the makers of the show. I loved The Clangers. Such an iconic TV show, and I would love it if my Sweep could of inspired their speech. May I add the fact I don't refer to myself as 'Sooty's Dad' but as 'Sooty's brother', only Harry was 'Sooty's Dad'.

As well as your dad who or what influenced your childhood? My friends and family where such an influence and pushed me into doing what I did. When my brother declined the offer of being Sooty's new friend, I felt pressured into receiving the role, although being super excited. I had plans to leave in around 1986, but it was audiences that kept me going up until 1998.

How daunted were you taking over the reigns? As mentioned before, very excited although extremely nervous. Questions like "Will the children like the new Harry?" And "Will I be as good as my father?" where echoing my mind. If I hadn't accepted the job, I wouldn't be where I was today. I love my life, and wouldn't change it for anything.

Have you ever injured your wrist in any way? For a short time in the 80s I had a unknown form of arthritis in my arm and it stopped me from being the puppeteer of Sooty. After a while, it ran off and was never to be seen again, although I do occasionally receive shooting pains in both hands and my finger tips.

Having decided to retire, how much of a change was it - for Sooty? I think the series changed a lot when I left and I don't think Sooty was ever the same. I love Richard Cadell and he couldn't be any better of a presenter. At first, I never thought I would be able to let Sooty Heights go forward, I thought "No, I can't let Sooty leave me" but there's some decisions in life that you regret at first but support now.

Was there family tensions along the way and looking back now, was it still worth it all? There where tensions during the 80s when my Dad continued touring with Sooty as I was angry he wasn't resting. He left for his health, but unfortunately, he grew attached to Sooty. I remember when I was around 12, I asked my Dad for a help with some homework, and I got a simple 'No' back, because he was to busy playing with Sooty. I remember going on holidays and him drilling holes in the suitcases so Sooty could breath on the way there. He would even cook a meal for Sooty on a night, and sleep with him by his side. But without that, Sooty wouldn't be who he is today and I think all these hiccups over the years provided strength to keep flowing.

When you teamed up with Sooty again in 2011 did you get any pangs to come back more permanently? Let's start by saying I was SO HYPER. I couldn't sleep on a night knowing I would be appearing again. I knew, I couldn't take Richard away from Sooty after such a short time, although I was considering appearing in a few more episodes of Sooty in the future. If any readers would like to know if I'm returning to Sooty permanently, well, that's a maybe, but most probably a no. But, don't let down your hopes. I may see you in the future on CITV. Just keep watching. You never know.

How would you like people to remember your time with Sooty? I think the answer is obvious. I would love people to remember me on Sooty, and all 1,086 followers on Twitter (as of November 2012) do. I hope people have as many memories of Sooty with me than I do.

What advice would you give to budding puppeteers? Never give up hope. Stay strong. You WILL succeed.

And the big question - what does Sooty actually sound like?? Sooty, well, he sounds amazing. Someday I hope for all of you to hear his voice and be inspired by his beautiful words. I can tell you one thing, he can bloody talk for England. He never shuts up. But for now, all you can do is imagine what he sounds like.

Where can readers see you singing? If viewers follow my Twitter @Matthew_Corbett I occasionally release dates on there but mostly I perform around Lymm, where I live.

What have you done since leaving Sooty in 1998? I've been obviously performing and let's just say I've lost my voice more than a few times. I also have had amazing times with my wife, family and friends and have only recently got back from a wonderful holiday in Florence, Italy. I also spend 24/7 watching gameshows and creating quiz's about them on my Twitter feed. I also recently started a weekly quiz called "Corbetts Quiz" its held every Saturday at 7pm on @CorbettsQuiz Twitter account. Great prizes to be won! (I don't want to sound like an advertisement but...) If you follow my Twitter you will be truly satisfied with the tweets you read!! Thank you for asking me these questions and I hope the readers enjoy the rest of the book.

Matthew Corbett

LEE CORNES

MR. HANKIN - GRANGE HILL, MR BEAN: THE ANIMATED SERIES, TUGS,

I wonder what Ofsted would have made of Grange Hill? It was a tough old time for one of its teachers, Mr. Hankin (detention if you make fun of his name!) Lee played the role for 12 years but, in a case of life imitating art, he taught at real schools too. Lee is the head writer of the animated Mr. Bean series and has several other writing projects up his sleeve, but his first love has been comedy.

I've always clowned around and in the sixth form, organised revues. Then, even though I pursued a geography/biology degree course, I got properly involved with comedy, our group being the first in Birmingham University's history to take a comedy show to the Edinburgh Festival. After that I knew I'd want to try acting/comedy. My influences were 'The Phil Silvers Show', 'The Lucy Show', Tony Hancock, Max Wall, 'Do Not Adjust Your Set', Peter Cook and Dudley Moore and The Pythons.

I was proud of the fact that, apparently, in polls of young viewers, Mr. Hankin was always well liked – probably the secret to his longevity! I enjoyed his comic aspects as well as his well meaning nature, even though he was quite naïve and earnest. His character became less of a stereotype science nerd though, emerging towards the end, a more rounded person.

I enjoyed carrying the storyline about testicular cancer for its importance in educating young men on this imprtant issue. It also stretched my acting abilities, exploring and testing Hankin's character.

As for what Mr. Hankin is doing now, I think he would probably have taken early retirement, hacked off with the way the teaching profession has become obsessed with results and targets rather than with the celebration of the wonder of science. Or maybe he'd be in prison for murdering an Ofsted inspector!

We almost always had fun, the staff room characters bonding both on and off set. The only thing I think I could be accused of was corpsing (laughing) on occasions.

I actually used to teach at Robertsbridge whilst being in Grange Hill at the same time. The idea that their science teacher in real life was a fictional science teacher on the telly often confused some of the students – some (I kid you not) thinking that they were somehow now in Grange Hill, rather than their own school. The more astute ones used to ask 'Why are you teaching here when you're on the telly?' A tough one to answer, to be sure. They seemed to think that everyone on TV earned a fortune. In any case, any kudos from being on TV quickly wore off and I soon became just another member of staff. I have continued teaching when it suits me, mostly in a special needs school for some years aswell as an EBSD school also.

Lee Cornes

I've worked on other shows such as 'The Young Ones' and as Dick Head, the barman, in 'Bottom' with Rik Mayall and Adrian Edmondson. They were very supportive of the suporting actors and both the rehearsals and the recording were great fun as it always felt like a team show. Rik was always trying to find the funniest way to do things.

It's hard to say if compering at a comedy club in front of a lively audience is harder than teaching a classroom of rowdy kids. It depends. At least you can say what you like to a comedy audience, but of course, as a teacher, your responses to tricky situations are necessarily very considered. Also, you see the same kids day in, day out, whereas that night's audience clears off never to be seen again. Definitely more fun being in front of an audience, though.

I found out that the comedian Sean Lock considers me to be an influence. I'm honoured and flattered by it and that he liked my act. Thanks Sean! Without a doubt he's always one of my favourite comedians, too.

As for highlights, I used to be part of a revue show called the 'Wow Show' in which four of us did what the hell we liked on stage, which I always found exhilarating and liberating. I enjoyed the TV sitcoms I've been involved in as well as appearing on ice (I can't skate) with Torvill and Dean on their national tour!

Lee Cornes

DICK & DOM

DICK AND DOM IN DA BUNGALOW, THE LEGEND OF DICK & DOM,
DIDDY MOVIES, DA DICK AND DOM DIARIES, SPLATALOT, HOOPLA

They may be 'diddy' but these two are modern day giants of children's television. After bursting onto the scene in their madcap messy BAFTA winning bungalow they've gone on to create a number of equally popular shows including the prophetically titled 'The Legend of Dick and Dom' as they are now Legends of Kids TV! So, please doff your caps and say 'bogies' and 'sloppy flap crackers' for messrs Richard McCourt and Dominic Wood.

Who were your legends of your own childhoods?

Phillip Schofield, Tommy Boyd, Timmy Mallet and Gilbert the Alien.

Where and when did you first meet?

Met at the BBC (Dick was a runner, Dom doing magic on a show called the Friday Zone). Became mates and then the on screen partnership started in 1997.

What have been your favourite live moments?

Cutting open the belly of a large salmon and sticking it on a girls head. (Da Bungalow). Da Bungalow was Live on Saturday mornings and they were some of the best times.

Are there any celebs that deserve to be covered in creamy muck muck!?

Rachel Stevens, she came on the show and refused to be creamy muck mucked.

What's been your most interesting fan mail?

Someone sent us there entire weekly food shop!

Who is the worst corpser?

Dick says Dom. Dom says Dick.

Where was your favourite 'bogies' venue and which was the most nerve-wracking?

Either Glasgow library or Madame Tussauds. Most nerve-racking at a play in an Exeter theatre - they had no idea we would be there.

Can you describe each other in just 5 words?

Dick (on Dom) Short mental paranoid balding man

Dom (on Dick) nose, eyes, teeth, hair, lips

Which of your shows have given you the most satisfaction?

Da Bungalow - 5 years of award winning ridiculous slap about.

What can you tell me about your next series/upcoming projects?

Absolute Genius looks into the lives of inventors/genius's - more highbrow but with that inevitable D&D style. HOOPLA! our new entertainment show set in a circus/fairground is like the bungalow's big bro (and made by Steve Ryde the Producer of Da Bungalow, the legend of D&D and Diddy movies!)

Dick & Dom

You can keep up to date with Dick & Dom's current shows at www.dickndom.com

JOHNNY EDWARD
METAL MICKEY

John Edward has worked in the music industry since first starting out as a lead guitarist with Davy Jones (David Bowie) and the Manish Boys at the tender age of 17. He now prefers to be called Johnny. He's had a long and varied career; edited his own magazine 'Beat 64', was among the first breed of pirate Deejays on Big L (Radio London) an independent record producer, manager/agent of Edison Lighthouse and gave birth to Hollywood recording studios.

Johnny's biggest success in the music industry was as producer, publisher, co-writer (with his wife Sue) and video director of the infamous Renee & Renato international number one chart topper 'Save Your Love' which sold 2 million copies, but out of all that he also gave birth to a famous tin robot, but how did Metal Mickey come to life?

I produced a record called 'Lollipop' (an oldie by the Mudlarks originally) by a harmony group called 'Junior High and The Rockets' and needed top find a label to release it.

I played it to the PYE records A&R man John Schroeder. He'd just had an American Number One hit with 'Sleepy Shores' and Pictures Of Matchstick Men by Status Quo was beginning to tickle.

He liked it but thought it needed to be different to stand out from the crowd. I pondered and fresh from a dream of robots, I awoke to imagine a robot singing the song!

I treated the voice with a gizmo called a 'vocoder' and the record was mixed and offered around to various labels. They were all interested but wanted to see the robot! I even had drawings made. Eventually, EMI offered a deal but waited a year to release the track. Unfortunately, I didn't dent the charts as they gave it zero promotion.

Mickey took approx six months to build and was made by Andy Thompson. Several paintings were done and various names considered including 'Metal Box Kid'.

The then Metal Box Kid

Over the years Mickey has met so many celebrities... If only I had a larger flash drive in my noddle! Bill Oddie, Robbie Coltrane, Irene Handl, Gary Shail, Michael Dolenz, Opal Bonfante (Sky), Kenny Everett, Larry Grayson and has appeared on Game For A Laugh with Jeremy Beadle, Henry Kelly, Mathew Kelly, and Sarah Kennedy, Esther Rantzen's That's Life and The Russ Abbot Show.

Mickey's own sit-com happened because I was watching telly and saw a friendly looking guy called (I thought) Humphrey Barclay, I later found out that it was actually Humphrey Burton! My letter to Mr Barclay, however, (and the tape I sent him of MetalMickey's TV appearances) elicited a reply. Soon we were recording a pilot and almost as quickly, a six part series. Micky Dolenz was brought in by Humphrey as was Colin Bostock Smith.

It was great fun. The naughty boys in the LWT crew once stuck a length of stuck together paper cups on Mickey lower abdomen. The audience laughed so much, I couldn't think what Mickey had said to make them respond that way.

Irene Handl was nice when she wasn't being grumpy, but sadly, not the woman you saw on screen. That was an act, no doubt, albeit a convincing one. She idolised a tiny cat sized dog, which she carried in a basket everywhere she went.

She spoke like a Duchess, with overly pronounced vowels. Could have played a Queen, but her 'stock in trade' was a cockney 'street' voice.

Irene Handl

Mickey loves to boogie boogie and he would definitely consider Strictly Come Dancing. He might have difficulty with a quickstep, but judging wouldn't be too much of a problem. Also, he would easily slip into Simon Cowell's shoes on X Factor!

I have to say that the highlight of Mickey's career so far is being asked to feature in this book.

Johnny Edward

To relive more of Mickey and Johnny's careers and to book Metal Mickey for your event please visit www.metalmickey.com

SIMON FARNABY

HORRIBLE HISTORIES

Horrible Histories is massive. I mean, really massive and hugely popular with children and adults alike. The main gang of Mathew Baynton, Martha Howe-Douglas, Simon Farnaby, Jim Howick, Laurence Rickard & Ben Willbond have done wonders (along with the writers) bringing Terry Deary's creation to life winning a raft of awards along the way including a British Comedy Award, a first for a children's television programme, and if they didn't believe it then, they went on to win it a second time to make sure! Here's a Q&A with the man behind the Grim Reaper...

Who have been your favourite characters to play from an acting point of view?

I like stupid death because it's a character I did right from the start so I know him so well I only have to partially learn my lines and busk the rest.

and from a historical point of view?

Caligula was fun because it's a part played by many fine actors in the past and of course historically he was infamous. During the first take I thought I'd gone way over the top. Then our director steve said "bigger, go as mad as you can" I thought, "ok, this job is not the same as others"

With it's range of characters, songs, comedy, dressing up, would you say HH is an ideal job?

Which leads me onto this. It is the ideal job in that you get to goof around with your mates in silly wigs and outfits and get to do as many silly voices as is humanly possible. But we film so much stuff it's hard work and exhausting. No matter how much fun we have, by the end we're all suffering from exhaustion.

What was it like performing at the Royal Albert Hall?

Very surreal. So much history there. When we came out to dothe four George's I realised why people join boy bands, to get that unadulterated adulation, the screaming and hysterics. It also made me realise why I've never been in a boy band.

What do you enjoy most about working on HH?

Messing around with the others and finding something that makes them laugh.

How hard is it to keep a straight face, and who is the worst corpser?

I'm pretty good at the straight face stuff. I think if you're on the verge of corpsing tats when you're onto something magic, but if you blow every take pissing yourself you'll never get it down. Jim is probably the worst corpser, followed by matt who often corpses himself. But all of us get the giggles at some stage or other especially towards the end of the shoot.

Simon Farnaby

What do you think is the secret to HH's success?

I think it's very unpretentious . It's funny and you learn stuff. Parents Actually likE their kids watching it on tv. There's not many tv shows you can say that about.

How good was your own history knowledge before working on HH?

Terrible. Now it's not so bad. And I now know some stuff, like the west indies is so called becaue Columbus thought he'd landed in India! I always wondered why it was called that. Now I know.

How hard did you all party after winning the British Comedy Award?

Well I ended up in rehab the first time, then martha did the second time. Larry has promised he'll go if we win a third.

There's a lot of wee, poo and vomit on HH, do you have a favourite?

We all prefer vomit because there are funny ways of throwing up. There's not many funny ways to wee.

What's been your favourite sketch so far?

There's one in this series where Jim kicks a chicken into the sea. I simply couldn't get through it for laughing. I only have two lines in it but it's my favorite in terms of making me laugh.

Do you think HH might create a sea-change in terms of funding for home-grown, quality children's programming?

No idea. There should be a change. No one in kids TV makes ANY money. That much I do know. The budgets are tiny.

Did playing William Burke in HH make you want to be in the Burke & Hare movie?

Did I play Burke in HH? Oh yes. In Matt's song. Wow, I didn't know that was a character I played twice.

How far do you think HH can go?

Not much further in its current format but maybe movies?

Do you think that HH might start to influence how subjects are taught in schools?

I'm sure it will. Ive heard it just gets played in some schools when the teachers run out of ideas.

What are you most proud of in your career so far?

Probably Bunny and the Bull. A little known british film by the director of the mighty boosh. Funnily enough a lot of horrible histories fans have started buying it on DVD .

Do you have a favourite stupid death?

We film so many in a day I can never remember them. Moliere I think. Didn't he die onstage during a production of the hypochondriac. It sounds like I just made that up but. Think it's true.

And finally, If you had a choice of your own stupid death, how would you like to go?

No one in their right mind would wish a stupid death upon themselves. Strangled by an elephants trunk? I'm only saying that because the chances of that actually happening in some ironic twist is zero. Or is it!?

Simon Farnaby

KEITH FIELD
A HANDFUL OF SONGS

"We've got a handful of songs to sing you..." went the refrain and over many years Keith certainly did that, predominantly with Maria Morgan and they proved to be an extremely popular partnership. It was the brainchild of inspirational producer Muriel Young but what memories does this clean living musician have of those times and of Auntie Mu?

Muriel Young was a wonderful lady. One day she said to me 'Keith, I've got this idea for a TV programme and I want you to write the scripts because you have the sense of humour of a 5 year old child!'

There were three children's programmes coming out of Granada Television at that time, one was 'Clapperboard' with Chris Kelly, who is my idol. I used to say to him 'I want to be Chris Kelly when I grow up!' He was just a brilliant presenter, so professional and such a lovely chap. It was the only children's film programme at that time. Then there was 'Lift Off with Ayshea' Ayshea was the singer in my band. She's also my son's Godmother. For the first 13 weeks of 'Lift Off' my band was live in the studio and we backed the singers because the unions at the time didn't want people to mime to backing tracks and wanted live music, but the trouble was they didn't know how to record a live band for the show in the studios at Granada. They were the same engineers who were doing 'Coronation Street' who used the same microphones but it was just a disaster. They recorded them all on a reel to reel tape and you couldn't hear anything, it was just an awful thing to do. The third programme was 'The 5 O'Clock Clu'b with Wally Whyton. Muriel was incredibly popular and was originally a children's TV presenter. 'The 5 O'Clock Clu'b featured two puppets, Pussycat Willum and Fred Barker. I think Wally voiced Fred Barker and the other was voiced by Ivan Owen, who went on to do Basil Brush. They were all a little gang who knew each other and we were the next generation to come along.

It was from appearing on 'Lift Off' that I met Muriel Young because she produced all the programmes and that's when she told me of her idea for 'A Handful of Songs'. She actually wrote it for Wally Whyton who was presenting Country Club on BBC Radio 2 but was too busy to do 'A Handful of Songs' so Muriel asked me to do it. I was playing an electric guitar on 'Lift Off' and Muriel asked me if I had an acoustic guitar 'Of course I have' I said. I hadn't actually, but I went straight out and bought one!

The idea was that Tony Hart (of Take Hart) got all the talented kids paintings and we got the ones that weren't as good, but that was lovely because if a child would do one blob of paint their mum would write on the bottom that it was Humpty Dumpty, which was fine. When that was seen on the telly there would be mums up and down the country saying to their children 'come on, you can do better than that.' When I was writing the scripts I'd have the pictures all over the floor and would work through them trying to find a funny little theme to run through each show. The kids loved sentences that started with the same letter, so there would be some alliteration and play on words and the occasional jokes for the adults because I realised there were lots of mums with children on their laps and from the letters we got, a lot of people on shift work and students and unemployed people who were also watching it, as they would write in and say 'we have a right laugh' and 'thank you for the programme, it's great fun. It takes me back to my childhood.'

"We've got a handful of songs to sing you, can't stop my voice when it longs to sing you..."

It was a popular programme. Amazingly one Christmas we had 5 million viewers, which was the biggest we ever had. It was broadcast on a Friday which was Christmas Eve, so a lot of people were at home watching it that day.

I did 379 episodes of 'A Handful of Songs' in total over 8 or 9 years. It started off as a 5 minute programme in the Granada area and then it went nationwide. The other regions liked it and wanted to broadcast it, so it turned into a 11 minute and 5 second programme (as that was the length I had to write the scripts to).

There was one amazing day in particular that's seared in my memory. We did two programmes, I'd written the scripts, it was put on the autocue, everything had been rehearsed, all the pictures were put on the right easels – it was quite a technical programme with all the pictures, then Muriel popped her head over the directors bar and said 'We've got a lot more VTR time, so why don't we do another programme?' and I said 'but Muriel, we haven't got a script' to which she just said 'Oh, you can make it up, can't you darling?' So, we quickly got our heads together with all the stage crew, picked some more pictures and put them on the easels and decided who would do what. It was only 11 minutes so we remembered it all and we just waffled like we normally waffle, but with the kind of style we had between us, and we recorded the whole programme without a script!

Working at Granada was lovely. It didn't feel like you were in showbusiness, it was more like a bunch of chums just having fun. In those days Sidney Bernstein was the chairman and David Plowright was the Managing Director and it was a real local TV service – now it's part of a big conglomerate. It was Manchester and Liverpool's own little, local station, so it was a wonderful atmosphere to work in up there. We mixed with all the 'Coronation Street' people, the dust bin men, those on 'Brideshead Revisited'. It was like being in a great big family. We all ate together in the canteen and it was a lovely job to do and lovely to work for Muriel Young.

I'm sure there's a lot of backstabbing that goes on in television but Muriel protected us from everything. If Maria or I were concerned about something we just spoke to Muriel and she sorted everything out so it ran like clockwork. There was probably some real wheeler dealing going on somewhere behind the scenes, but we were completely left out of it.

When Mu retired, some other new broom came into Granada to run the programmes and his first act was to cancel everything that Mu had done, so we ended up without a job. I've no idea what

he did afterwards or if he came up with any other programmes. As I was doing some exhibitions in my spare time I ended up doing that and Maria went on to play Evita in the West End. 'A Handful of Songs' was her first singing job ever, so to go on to do that was absolutely brilliant. Most of the people in the West End have been to stage school and learnt to sing and dance, but to do it without that amount of training is absolutely phenomenal. Maria still looks the same – I think she must have an oil painting in the attic! I definitely look my age now but she's very well preserved!

In actual fact, after 'A Handful of Songs' Biddy Baxter rang me up and asked if I would like to come and meet her to talk about joining 'Blue Peter', so I went round the studios and met the other people and it was going ever so well. We went out to lunch and she asked me how old I was and I said I was 31 and she said that I can't join 'Blue Peter', I was too old! She thought that on the television I looked quite young and I always looked younger than I am. Having been in the music business since the age of 16 I've never ever taken drugs or been on the drink. I suppose I was a bit more preserved than some of my colleagues! I did quite a few TV commercials at one time because they wanted someone who could play the guitar and looked like he was convincing but didn't look like he'd been on drugs all night! Some of my colleagues in the music biz looked around 20 years older than they are! It's not a healthy lifestyle, but some can treat that lifestyle as a job.

Muriel was known as 'Auntie Mu' which is what she was called on 'The 5 O'Clock Club'. She passed away in 2001 and there was a memorial service for her at St. Pauls in Covent Garden. All the people who'd ever worked with her on all the programmes she'd produced were there and we all got together and did a little show on the alter (It happens a lot at St. Pauls, so the vicar was saying). They could move to the West End with all the tributes they have for people that are performed there. We sung 'A Handful of Songs' and talked about our work with Mu and another group from 'Get it Together', which was another of her programmes, came up and there was a bit from 'Lift Off'. It was really nice because she so loved. A very popular lady.

As a musician I released a couple of singles in 1968. 'The Day that Wore Broke Out' and 'Stop Thief' which I wrote for Georgie Fame. It sounded like him and I ended up putting it on my B-side. 'The Day that Wore Broke out' was written by Mike D'Arbo from The Mannfreds. I went to see them at the St. Albans Arena a few years ago. Paul Jones and Mike D'Arbo were the two main singers doing all their own songs. Mike sang all the other hits he'd written for other people like 'Build Me Up Buttercup' and after the show I went to see him because they were signing autographs in the foyer and I said 'I'm sorry mine wasn't a hit' and he said 'Keith! I've not seen you in 40 years!' and he also said that it was a lovely record. It's good to see them still working. I gave up playing years ago and started an exhibition business which my son has now taken over. He asks me to do things occasionally when they get busy and pulls me out of retirement. The songs are on YouTube now. All the girls at school when I go to pick my grandson up on a Monday say "Oh, I've seen you on YouTube" After years of anonymity with no one knowing what I used to do, now everybody knows what I used to do!

Looking back on those times was incredible. There was a band I was in called The Blue Aces who came from Limerick in Ireland, and they were a band with brass, a bit like The Commitmants, but 20 years before them, and we used to do soul music and for a while we were the only people playing soul. That's how I met Gino, who was still in the US Air Force. He went on to form the Ram Jam Band and I joined. I also had my own band in London.

Away from music I've always been a great Aston Martin enthusiast. I've restored a couple and at that time of 'A Handful of Songs' I had a red Aston Martin and I used to drive up to Granada at 3am in the morning to record the programme. Of course, in those days, they didn't seem to be very hot on speeding and I could get from London to Manchester in 2 and a quarter hours. It was a very enjoyable job altogether. Very very hard work but wonderful and writing the scripts was huge fun.

With children's television today a lot of older people complain about how loud some of it is, zapping ray guns, explosions and for young kids some of it is just rubbish. There are programmes like 'Peppa Pig' and the 'Mickey Mouse Club' and 'Tigger & Pooh' with Darby that all have lovely values and clever characterisations. It should be about growing up and childhood things and you just hope that you don't park your kids in front of stuff that isn't that good to watch. When you try and calm a kid down you don't give them that drink that makes them hyperactive you need something that calms them down and makes them smile. They just want to sit on your lap and have a cuddle, don't they? I think some people use it as a way of going off and doing other things while they put the kid in front of the television, but you've got to be with them while watching it and sharing it.

From my career 'A Handful of Songs' is an obvious highlight. I wrote it and thought of it as my show, really, but I also did a lovely tour of America with Peter Noone of Hermin's Hermits. I really enjoyed that because I got together a really marvellous band of American musicians from Denver, Colorado. They were college kids but were just so talented. I wrote an act for Peter with lots of Herman's Hermits stuff in it and also some Jacques Brel so he could make a name for himself as a solo artist. We toured for about 3 weeks and I got so homesick because my kids were young and I said to Peter 'I've done the job, I've launched you off, can I go home now please???' so despite having an almost permanent job as a musical director I wanted to get home and realised that's not what I wanted to do for a living, but it was such a nice experience going around America and, of course, it wasn't riotous, we just lived a normal life. Peter's a nice lad and he was with his wife and it was very pleasant. You hear stories of being on tour with Led Zeppelin for example, but we weren't like that at all. The resident band we had in London for 7 years were all just nice family people. No drugs. Nothing stronger than black coffee! I handed over the exhibition company to my son on my 65th birthday and it's such a relief not to do all the organisation, but it's nice to go to Cannes for the occasional job!"

Keith Field

To find out more about Marketing Services International you can check out their website www.marketingsupportint.com

2 PETER FIRMIN

BAGPUSS, NOGGIN THE NOGGIN THE NOG, IVOR THE ENGINE,
THE CLANGERS, POGLES WOOD, BASIL BRUSH

Peter had a wonderful partnership with the late Oliver Postgate. Being the artist who drew the pictures, designed the sets and built the models they produced a number of classic programmes such as Noggin the Nog, Ivor the Engine, Pogles Wood, The Clangers and Bagpuss - the pink cat who was originally intended to be marmalade. Peter's daughter Emily also made a memorable contribution!

At what age did you first start drawing and what was the very first model you made?

My mum sat me and my brother down on rainy days with a pencil and paper. I must have been as young as 4 or 5. My father worked in the Telegraph Office of the Railway and he always brought spare paper home.

Before and during the war (I was born in 1928 and my brother Lewis in 1927) we made models of the new aircraft that were being made and got our plans from the Aeroplane Magazine of the new British and German planes. As there was no plastics or kits, we made our models by wittling bits of wood. I still have Lewis's model of a Spitfire and a Seaplane. I also made string puppets, although not very successfully.

Did your parents encourage your creative side?

Yes, my father had two hobbies. He mended watches and he liked calligraphy, so some of the timetables which he wrote out for the ticket office at Parkeston Quay Station were very elegant. And my mother did quite nice flower drawings but was frustrated by the demands of being a mother and wife in the depression and in wartime. So we all inherited their talents and they encouraged us to develop them.

When you were creating characters where did your inspirations come from?

Oliver Postgate first created characters such as Ivor the Engine, and Alexander the Mouse. I did the drawings, mostly trying to visualise what Oliver imagined. Later when I tried developing my own ideas for stories, the inspiration came from museums and books. For instance, Noggin the Nog is based on the Isle of Lewis chessmen in the British Museum. I thought of it as a love story, with the "hero" Noggin going off on an adventure to find his bride. The inspiration for the style of the storytelling came from the great Norse Sagas, "Beowulf" and "The Battle of Maldon". My writing talents were not sufficient to carry it off, but as Oliver also found the Chessmen interesting, and as we wanted a new subject to present to the BBC he developed my outline stories and added many new characters and the films became quite successful. I did all the drawings.

As for Bagpuss, my other creation, the seed of that character was a cat in a book by the famous Czech animator, Jiri Trnka. I saw it in a magic storytelling relationship with a little girl of about the same age as my youngest daughter Emily, but again, Oliver and I eventually decided that the setting would be Emily's shop. Of course, it was Emily who played the part (only in still photographs) in the Bagpuss films. Other characters came from various places. Gabriel the Toad was a real toad in the basement garden where Joan and I lived in Twickenham. I first made him as a puppet for the programme called "The Musical Box" which I devised with Rolf Harris in 1959 and later with Wally Whyton. The main live animations were nursery rhymes, but we found we needed singing puppets. Later he was chosen for the cast of Bagpuss. Madeleine the ragdoll was based on a Nightie Case that my wife Joan made for the daughters. Yaffle the Woodpecker was based on a real green woodpecker and replaced another character that the BBC did not like.

Oliver came up with the "Mouseorgan" and all the mice.

When we were asked for a spacey series for little children, we trawled through our earlier books and found a moonmouse landing in the horsetrough of Noggin's Castle. We brought him up to date and called him a Clanger, found out that he lived with his family on a little blue moon somewhere not too far away in space, and the Clangers were born.

How much free reign did you have when making Basil Brush?

I was actually asked to make two tiger-cub puppets as part of an out-of-work circus act called "The Three Scampies" devised by Ivan Owen, Wally Whyton for Associated-Rediffusion's Smalltime programmes. I thought that they were far too big for glove-puppets so suggested a fox and a hedgehog. I made the puppets but they were named by the creators of the stories. Because they could not pay me for all the work, it was suggested that I just was paid £12 plus a payment every time they were used. This meant that I still owned the puppet. Luckily I still have rights and benefit from Basil's revived success!

Ivan Owen was known to avoid the limelight to protect Basil's magic, what are your memories of Ivan?

Ivan had ambitions to be an actor, but found his real talents fulfilled when he had the puppet on his hand and could be concealed under the table. Before Basil, he had designed and made several puppets, for "Huff-Puff Junction" and "All at Sea". He was a talented model maker, making all the sets as well as the puppets. He and his family were and still are great friends and it was always a laugh to work with him.

Was the Clangers manner of speaking influenced by Harry Corbett's Sweep?

No, definitely not. Oliver had the idea of using swanny whistles for these characters who lived on a planet far away. They obviously would not speak English, and Oliver was convinced that the children would understand every squeak. But the ladies of the BBC insisted that the viewers would not know what was going on, so Oliver added a narration to explain the story. When we visited a puppet festival in Germany, Oliver showed the films without the narration and the German audience said that they were speaking perfect German!

How long did it an episode of Bagpuss take to animate?

The whole series of 13 films took Oliver about a year and a half to make. He was animating on his own, starting with the sound tracks, so I suppose each episode took about a month, although they varied according to the work involved.

Bagpuss's colour proved to work a treat, but when you first saw the colour of the cloth what did you think? Were you tempted to have it re-made?

No, it was a stroke of luck that the colour was so unusual. I believe that we should accept all those unexpected chances that occur.

How long did Professor Yaffle take to make and what kind of wood was used?

I never really time myself. It takes as long as it takes to get it right. It was a mixture of plywood and blocks of pine.

What were the best parts of your working relationship with Oliver?

We absolutely trusted each other, and respected each other's opinions even when they differed. We never had any complicated contracts or agreements. Luckily, we were on the same wavelength and always arrived at a successful result after quite serious discussions about the way a film was made.

Was it evident from an early age that Emily (and your other children) had got your artistic genes?

Emily works with her partner Justin making their amazing papier Mache creations and printing linocuts and cards. All my girls inherited the genes from me and especially from their mother who has always been busy with her bookbinding and textile work, never idle. They are all good workers.

Which part of the film making process did you enjoy the most?

When I had made all the puppets and sets in my studio (ex cowshed) and drawn the titles, all of which I enjoyed, and Oliver had animated the first episode and received it back from the film processors, we would gather in Oliver's studio (ex pigstye) to watch the rushes. It was always an exciting surprise.

Out of all the programmes you made which ones gave you the most satisfaction and why?

The puppet programmes were most rewarding as a world was created with the things I made. They did not depend on my drawings like Ivor and Noggin did, but became believable magical worlds. The earliest, "Pogles Wood" was exciting as it was the first for which I had built sets. Oliver had learnt of the pitfalls of live outdoor animation with "The Pingwings" and the ghostly footsteps and moving shadows persuaded him to do the Pogles mostly in the Barn. Of course by the time we had started Bagpuss, Oliver was much more skilled and the result can still be watched with pleasure, although like Clangers, it was made by "Stop-frame" with his 16mm Bolex camera.

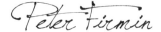

Noggin the Nog

PHIL FLETCHER
CBBC, SCOOP, HACKER TIME

Phil is from Wigan. You'll usually find Phil behind a desk, but it's a very different sort of office job, for Phil is the handler of the face of CBBC - Hacker T. Dog. A life touring his puppet show on the cabaret circuit has stood him in good stead and Hacker is a character he can really get his teeth into. Some say that animals can start to look like their owners and although Phil doesn't yet have a wet nose the similarities are greater than you may think...

I've been puppeteering since I was about 3. The first puppet that I had was an Emu puppet. Rod Hull and Emu are among my biggest influences, I still consider Rod Hull to be one of the best puppeteers that I've ever seen, you really believe that Emu is an independent being. I went to a fancy dress party on Hallowe'en night as Rod Hull and Emu, so I got this big wig and top hat and a replica Emu that I made built onto a jacket complete with false arm but all the youngsters at the party didn't know who I was meant to be they thought I was Willy Wonka holding a turkey! I told them to google Rod Hull and stop asking me. They don't know they're born!

Phil as Rod Hull

The Muppets are superb. I was always aware that the lip synch was better on their shows than UK shows. Then I started making puppets with functioning mouths and flexible faces so you bring them to life in a more believable way.

When I was about 10 we acquired a sewing machine so I started making puppets out of cloth so that's when I started making proper puppets. And when I was 11, I started my own company, The Gluvets {Glove Puppets} in 1988 when I left primary school. In that six weeks holiday I started my own company, my dad made me a booth and I made the curtains for it and the sign for the front, I made a set of puppets and started doing kids birthday parties and started making money from puppets at 11. I did some shows at school for the other classes and sometimes for the textiles classes I'd take in puppets I'd made at home to show what you can do. I left school in 1993 and for the next 10 years I worked in factories, whilst at night building up the act and at weekends still doing kids parties and stuff. I got a couple of agents involved at this point and started doing cabaret at holiday camps and shopping malls and corporate events including Mercedes and I was also building puppets for other people at this point, some for telly, but mainly for stage and pantomimes. They were going all over the world at this point. I made stuff for Las Vegas TV and Polish television and eventually in 2002 the puppet work was getting that great I could pack in the day job. So it was then I went pro as a full time puppeteer and puppet builder and I've never stopped since.

The first thing I did with CBBC was in 2007 and I was asked to build a puppet for Ed & Oucho. It was a hamster that lived in a shredder, called the Shredder Hamster, kids would send in drawings and they'd get shredded and they'd cut to the Hamster where it would plot to try and take over the office. That's how I got my hand in, as it were.

The first character I performed for CBBC was Uncle Fronk who was Oucho's ginger loving uncle. He had a little bowler hat and ginger curly hair but he was obsessed with ginger; people who were ginger, ginger biscuits, ginger the root vegetable, ALL things ginger. That was a really fun afternoon of live TV, kids were sending in pictures of themselves with ginger hair and it was a positive way to do it. Then I carried on doing my cabaret shows. In 2008 CBBC rang me up to do an audition for the new character they were bringing in which ended up being Dunstan the Brain, who was a brain on a spring and he was brought in to replace Oucho who went away for 3 months to film 'Excellent Inventions' with Ed Petrie but I was too busy because cabaret was still really good, so another guy called Adam Carter ended up playing Dunstan. Then in 2009, the same thing happened again, they rang me up and asked if I would go and audition to play a new character while Oucho went away to film series 2 of Excellent Inventions and I was free that year because the credit crunch had hit the holiday camp circuit in the UK quite badly, so my diary was a lot emptier than before so I said, alright then.

They said they had this dog puppet who was in a show called 'Scoop' with Shaun Williamson. Now I'd never seen this show so I didn't know what to expect. He was lying around in a box and they thought of getting him out and using him to fill in this 4 month gap while Oucho's away. So I went down to London for the audition and saw Hacker for the first time. Andy Heath who performed Hacker in series 1 of Scoop went on to do 'Mongrels' and wasn't available to come in and do Hacker at this point, So I went to TV Centre and did my Hacker audition with Sam Nixon {from Sam and Mark} a couple of weeks later I got a call back to do a second audition with Dan Clarkson {from Dan & Jeff} who currently do Potted Potter, and doing really well on Broadway – which is irrelevant to this story! - It went really well and I got the job. It was a 4 month contract, which was brilliant so I thought I'd do 4 months on telly and then go back to doing cabaret and stick 'As seen on TV' on my cards and I could get more work, because that's all I was ever thinking of in the long term. About a month and a half into the 4 month contract doing live afternoons I was asked to go to Wimbledon with Hacker to do a VT about tennis with Sue Barker and co. and I think that really propelled Hacker into the big time because they played our CBBC Hacker at Wimbledon VT on BBC2 at the end of play instead of the tennis highlights and it projected Hacker into the stratosphere. He went massive then and you could feel it, there was a marked difference between the day before and the day after.

That contract came to an end and they gave me another 6 months, which was great, so I continued doing live afternoons with Iain Sterling, then we did new 'Scoop', so I did 26 episodes of that with Shaun Williamson and it did really well. In that Hacker spoke and walked upright, because prior to me doing Hacker he didn't speak. He was played almost as a real dog, on all fours. He only growled and barked. Hacker's popularity got bigger and bigger to the point where he ended up doing stuff for 'Children in Need', 'Red Nose Day' and guesting on other shows like 'Little Howard's Big Question' and all these little things led us to do a pilot for a show called 'Hacker's Howlers' which was basically going to be Hacker's version of 'You've Been Framed' then we started coming up with ideas for new sketches and strands and that became 'Hacker Time' it became a chat/sketch show and we got guests in and brought in other puppets like Derek McGee and Wilf Breadbin who are my Gluvets characters I thought I could throw them into the mix. I also played Keith Teeth in one of the episodes. Series 1 was on the long list for BAFTA. It didn't make the short list, tragically, but it got down the top 10 before they reach the final 4 which isn't bad.

We got a second series of 'Hacker Time' which went out earlier this year {2012} to great reviews and great reactions and great viewing figures, got some lovely reviews in Radio Times and now they're talking about doing more things with Hacker, there's a lot of things in the pipeline and I think 2013 will be really big for him. I've been doing lots of appearances lately, such as Christmas light switch ons, Chris {Yonko} Johnson, Dodge and Hacker did Manchester's and 20,000 people were chanting "Hacker, Hacker" before we even went on stage.

When I took over Hacker it was virtually a blank canvas because Andy had played him like a real dog. So I just made him more and more like me; his birthday is my birthday, his favourite music is my favourite music, he's into musicals and shows tunes and so am I and I like meat paste and Hacker loves meat paste, so everything that Hacker does is just me, then you're never going to

Phil Fletcher

get caught out if you're in an interview or in an ad-lib situation so that's why Hacker works really well live and off the cuff, because anything that's asked of him, there's always an answer for it. I've worked live in front of hundreds and thousands of people over the years, so I know what works in front of a live audience I'm never stuck for a gag or something to say because I've more or less said everything over the years before. It's a great tool, you could never buy that training. I've worked with some shocking audiences and some brilliant ones. I've done Butlins, Haven, Pontins, all those and worked in most major theatres in the UK doing my act and touring.

I was saying before about Hacker being just me, that's what makes him real, even though he's a talking dog, it's 95% real. There's hardly any fiction in that character apart from the Sue Barker fascination, that's the only thing that's more or less fictional because I'm not a sports fan! But Hacker loves Sue, everything else is just me – all the little sarky lines he comes out with and all the little coughs he does and all the little weird things, that's just me and that's why I think he works so well because he's real even though he's a puppet dog.

One thing I've learned from doing puppet shows on the cabaret circuit is that you always have as many, if not more adults, watching you than kids, so I have always catered my act to entertain everyone watching and with Hacker I still do that. Iain and Hacker have got the same sense of timing and that's something we didn't plan because we didn't audition together. We got the jobs separately and were thrown together and within a couple of weeks we were doing live telly because it was coming up to half term. It's been very successful because within 6 months of being there Iain and Hacker were nominated for BAFTA as best presenters. I don't think any other puppeteer has ever been nominated for a BAFTA before.

I still do the odd Gluvets act, as it's good to keep your hand in. I used to do it full time and sometimes I did 2 a day. For example, on a Saturday I'd start of from here, Wigan where I come from (so does Hacker – that's another similarity between us!) and drive all the way down to Hastings and do the Pontins there at Rye, Cambersands then travel over to Hemsby and do one there and I'd literally work my way around the country and end up back at Blackpool on the friday night then go back down the following saturday and do it all again the longest stretch I did was 44 nights on the bounce without a night off. It's hard work but it's so much fun.

I've been doing Hacker for 3 and a half years now and I just love it so much. It's just a laugh, every day. Because of my style of improv and ad-libbing and the general way that character is, it's just a joy to do and even I don't know what's going to happen next – and I love that!

We were on the North West segments for Children In Need recently. Most of those segments were just me and Pudsey so I had to carry that and when I got there they were a bit worried, so I said 'don't worry, I do live links every day with a hard count in my ear, I can do this without any worries' so I did all the live links and they said to me at the end that that was the funniest Children In Need they'd ever done. I'd love to do more things like that for Comic Relief perhaps. The Wimbledon bit was the tipping point, for me, that was the point when Hacker went from being a Gordon the Gopher style puppet sidekick to becoming a TV presenter and star.

I've been doing some personal appearances lately, which I don't do that often, really. I'm normally only in that studio and there's nobody ever there so as a kids TV presenter you rarely interact with the kids or the audience generally, but having done live shows I know what kids like and what makes them laugh, but I'd not done that with Hacker before so when I did the Manchester lights switch

Phil with some of The Gluvets

on with The Wanted and Misha B, Hacker was getting a great reaction from the crowd. It was amazing. You don't expect it until it happens because normally when I'm at work I'm under that desk and I've just got a bit of MDF in front of me and Iain's legs, you literally feel like you're doing it for yourself. That's probably part of why it's so good because you don't think about the audience to much, you just forget they are there, until you face them, then you get the adoration for that character and you realise people DO love it.

I think Hacker could do any sort of programme, he's that sort of character. I've done a few radio things recently and I did a show called 'Retail Therapy' on BBC Radio Manchester. We recorded it live from Wigan Market Hall. There was a big audience of people and kids who'd come down from all over the country to see Hacker live and have their picture taken with. It was early morning and only an hours show from about 9am. It's funny already that Hacker's on radio. I think that works well. I always take the puppet in then you get the genuine reaction from the presenter rather than just me talking in a funny voice, it's better if they can watch the puppet. That show went down really well to the point where BBC Radio Manchester have asked us to do a Christmas morning radio show called 'A Merry Hacker Christmas' where Hacker's opening all his presents and Hacker's playing his favourite songs like 'Cotton Eyed Joe' and they're trying to get Sue Barker on the phone.

I'm also doing another radio programme called 'Blue Tuesday' which is a football programme. Now, Hacker has no interest in sport and no knowledge about it but they still want him on as a guest so he can offer nothing other than being weird and daft, but they still want it to happen so that tells me that he could do anything.

He was part of the CBBC alternative red button commentary for an England football game and it went viral worldwide. It trended worldwide on Twitter and Hacker got great reviews in all the national papers, it was in The Times and The Guardian, Chris Moyles was tweeting about it because his commentary got less listeners than ours apparently, but Hacker was more proud that the Wigan Evening Post mentioned him in the paper It said that he was more entertaining than Mark Lawrenson. Prior to that I'd done the Rugby World Cup commentary as Hacker which mainly consisted of Hacker saying 'oh, look, that mans got mud on his arm'.

Her Majesty The Queen and Prince Phillip came to officially open our studio last year and we heard from the Palace that the Queen wanted to meet the CBBC dogs because she has grandkids that are fans. She came to our studios and Hacker and Dodge did a routine for the Queen and she said 'that's very good, isn't it'. She loved it, she was laughing at Hacker and Dodge when they asked her if they could be her new corgis and that was on the world wide news.

I'm still keen to do more Hacker Time. Its funny when I'm filming a show because I stay in character all day. I'll meet the guests at the top of the day then I'll get under the desk. It takes 4 hours to film the studio segment of an episode and I more or less stay in character for the entire 4 hours so people will not

Keith Teeth

interact with me, they'll only interact with Hacker really, they just buy into it. Jenny McAlpine (Fizz from Coronation Street) came in with no preconceptions because she'd never heard of Hacker and had never seen it and we were saying 'right, later on you'll be dancing with a lemon' but within 20 minutes Hacker had her in the palm of his hand with his ways. Hacker's a big Coronation Street fan {so am i}, so I was talking to her about that and relaying anecdotes from 20 years ago, so it's brilliant what you can get away with really. In 'Hacker Time' I play Hacker, Derek McGee the director, Wilf Breadbin the van driver, Herman the work experience bloke and one of the cockroaches under the desk plus loads of one off characters and voice overs.

The funny thing with me, doing telly, is I never sought it out, it always came to me. I'm a realist. I know how impossible it is to get on telly, so I just assumed I'm never going to get on telly doing puppets so I made my own company and did it at gigs, because so long as I'm puppeteering, I've won, be it doing kids parties, be it doing Pontins or be it doing "Hacker Time" on telly, to me it's the same. I'm doing the same job. Luckily I did get on telly but you don't think you ever will because for me, it certainly feels like an impossible thing, so don't bother trying. I never did try, that was the funny thing, it always came to me. I started doing YouTube videos with The Gluvets just messing around doing jokes and miming to songs and I think that's where the CBBC guys first saw me, but I didn't put it on there with that intention.

Keith Teeth seems to be doing quite well. He's a character I do on Youtube. I thought I need to do something funny that makes me laugh, so I just did this crazy character. I'm quite a shy person really, I think most puppeteers are, that's why they're hiding under a desk.

Keith's shirt is one of Shaun Williamson's shirts from 'Scoop'. They had it made but they thought it might flare on camera so they didn't use it so I asked if I could have it at the end of the run and got this wig and had some teeth and started doing these videos and he seems to picked up a bit of interest. We've formed a band with a few of my mates who play instruments and we do the odd gig now called 'Keith Teeth and Friends' doing night clubs in Wigan to great reactions and reviews, and done some new bits on radio with him.

In series 1 of 'Hacker Time' there are load of pictures on the wall of various CBBC stars and I said to the producer 'If we do a series 2 can I have a picture of Keith Teeth on the wall?' He said 'Course you can, yeah. We'll not get a series 2!' Then of course we did get a second series so I called that favour up and I put a big picture of Keith on the set and he's in every episode and Keith makes a physical appearance in the Barney Harwood episode of 'Hacker Time', which I'm proud of.

Playing Hacker T. Dog on CBBC is a dream job for me it's just a laugh we get asked to do some nice, interesting things. Everyday is different you never know where it will lead. {Lead, another dog joke for you} Sniff.

Phil Fletcher

To find out more about The Gluvets please visit www.phil-puppets.com

Derek McGee

Not many entertainers can claim to have been in showbusiness for 50 years, but Keith Harris is one of them. Known globally for his ventriloquial skills and a shy green duck, Keith & Orville have entertained generations of children (and royalty) having been on Saturday evening television for over a decade and numerous Royal Command performances, plus they reached Number 4 in the UK charts in the early 80s, but what entertained the young Keith Harris in his childhood?

Ray Allen's T.V. show 'Tich and Quackers' and 'Crackerjack' entertained me as a child and the interest in ventriloquism grew as I was always telling jokes at school and the teacher told me to keep my mouth shut hence learning to speak without moving my lips.

I found Orville when he was an egg. He has always been shy and it was six months before he came out of his shell. Cuddles was inspired by the orangutans at Chester zoo. He was born in the sixties and had his own T.V. show 'Cuddles and Co.' in the 70's. Orville won't ever be coming out of nappies though, it's his gimmick and he can't find any trousers to fit him!

There have been some tough venues on the circuit. The working mens clubs in the North East in the 60's being the toughest. They had seen everything, if they liked you they let you live! But I did many T.V. shows before I got my own Saturday night variety show 'The Keith Harris Show' after being spotted by James Moyer head of B.B.C. light entertainment in 1981. The show ran until 1990 and then 'The Quack Chat Show' ran for another 3 years on Saturday evenings.

There have been lots of stories throughout my career but one of the first was whilst working with my first doll Charlie Chat. The string operating his mouth broke and we had to do the whole act with neither of us moving our lips. He was better at it than I was!

I have been in show business for 50 years and am also a script writer, producer and director and the highlights so far have been performing at the Royal Command performances and entertaining Prince William and Prince Harry at their Third birthday parties at Kensington Palace. At the moment I am working on a new pilot for a kids T.V. show and enjoying being rapper on You Tube - 'Giff Gaff K Orville'. We've had over 2 million hits so far!!

Keith Harris & Orville

BRIAN HERRING

MOPATOPS SHOP, WIZADORA, THE HOOBS, THE ANIMAL MAGIC SHOW, BOOKABOO, ANNABEL'S KITCHEN

After starting his puppetry career on the famous Spitting Image, Brian soon got into children's television, writing, voicing and performing on shows such as The Animal Magic Show, Mopatop's Shop, Wizadora as well as playing Hubba Hubba in The Hoobs. Brian's currently bringing Little Charley Bear to life on the West End stage.

I'd grown up in the 70's watching 'Vision On', 'The Muppet Show', 'Cholton and the Wheelies', 'Catweazle' and 'Bagpuss'. I was also obsessed with 'Star Wars'.

My mother worked in our local theatre and I decided at an early age I wanted to be on the stage.

I fled school as quickly as possible and started working as an actor at 18. A chance meeting in 1992 led me to an audition for 'Spitting Image' where I assured them I'd worked with puppets before... I hadn't.

I must have done something right as I was hired as an assistant puppeteer and after a training course where my teachers included Simon (Nobby the Sheep) Buckley, Nigel (Hartley Hare) Plaskett and the late great John (Playboard puppets) Thurtle (whose work I had adored as a small child) I was on national TV and in a show I had been watching for nearly a decade! Since then I've been waiting for someone to realise I've blagged my way in and throw me out on my ear!

After assisting my 'Spitting Image' colleges on shows like 'Cartoon Critters' and 'Roger & the Rotten Trolls', I became the last puppeteer to play Hangle on 'Wizadora'.

I got the part of Billy Nibbles (who I named after a friend's rabbit) on 'The Animal Magic Show' which starred a very young magician called Dominic Wood (whatever happened to him?) Dom and I did four series of that show and I wrote lots of the episodes. Billy had a lot of me in him and has been one of my favourite characters to perform.

Through both 'Spitting Image' and The Jim Henson company I've been lucky to work with most of the best puppeteers in the country. Each one brings their own energy and sense of humour to a set. I find it fascinating that many of them never intended to get into puppetry. Many (like myself) began as actors and fell into it. No two stories are the same and for that reason I have no idea what makes a successful puppeteer.

Brian with 'Little' Charley Bear

I just know that the ones I like to work with are, funny, have a good sense of drama, comedy and pathos. Can usually write their own material and are good in a crowd. That's one of the most important qualities. The ability to be stuck in a small space with people and get along with them.

Though they are all fun to be around, several names always raise a smile when I know they'll be working. Dave Chapman, whose work as Otis the Aardvark was funny to watch even as an adult. Dave set the standard for every CBBC puppet that would follow and he left behind him a very high bar.

Though I'd met him during Muppet treasure Island, and I'd guested in CBBC prez a couple of times, Dave and I didn't actually work together until 2007's 'Space Pirates', where he made me laugh for three weeks.

Dave is a quick witted, generous performer who is one of the best mimics I've ever come across.

Also Saturday morning TV stalwart Donald Austen with whom I had the pleasure of working on both 'Wizadora' and 'The Hoobs' is one of the funniest people I've ever seen pick up a puppet. Constantly amusing, Donald finds ways of working puppets that are both layered and nuanced. He will always be thinking of something new to try and he'll build on anything you throw at him.

Over the years I've found myself in some very odd positions... Some of them actually relating to work!

'Roger and the Rotten Trolls' was shot on location at Brimham Rocks in Yorkshire in the British 'summertime'. That was a wet shoot and it involved crouching in bushes and hanging off of strange craggy rock formations. I've also had to cram myself into dog kennels for CITV's 'Barking', under bus seats for a Virgin 1 campaign and more recently under the James Bond stage as black goop rained down on us whilst performing alien worms on Ridley Scott's 'Prometheus'. However, it's all part of the job and as long as it's not too dangerous, I'm happy to try anything!

Over the last few years I've been directing for the theatre as well and today saw the first day of rehearsals for 'Little Charley Bear and his Christmas Adventure' based on the hugely popular CbeeBees animation. The show runs from the 5th to the 25th of December at The Ambassador's theatre in London's west end and is written and directed by yours truly!

I've been 'messing about with puppets' for 20 years this year and I'm happy to say that I've never had a proper job.

Brian Herring

To find out more about Brian's career please visit www.laughingfish.co.uk

JEREMY HITCHEN

I was glued to the box whenever one of Gerry Anderson's creations was on and Terrahawks was no exception - Tiger Ninestein battling against the evil Zelda. I was totally immersed in it, even to the point of hoping the noughts would defeat the crosses in the end credits, so when I had the chance to meet up with the leader of the Terrahawks at the Foodies Festival at Hampton Court it was a definite Ten-Ten!

My dad was in the Royal Navy so I lived in Singapore, Malaysia, Cape Town and Belgium so when I was a kid I didn't have a great amount of television because we were in foreign lands and it was the 1960s and in those days when father came home you got told to go to bed as a 7 year old boy, so I used to listen to the World Service because I didn't like reading. It's funny that my life is reading scripts and I hated it back then.

I used to listen to 'Steptoe and Son' on the World Service and then I'd go and repeat it doing the impressions to my parents in the evening and for some reason Steptoe and Son just sticks in my mind. My mum and dad would have dinner parties and they would get me out of bed and say 'Oh come and do your Steptoe and Son thing.' Fortunately I could remember the storylines and give them about a 3 minute clip, which was all super and marvellous. After I finished in the luxury of the Royal Navy and living abroad I ended up going to school in Eltham, South London at a school called Crown Woods which is one of the biggest comprehensive schools in Britain, It was a very massive change to the privileged life I'd led as the son of a Navy officer. They did a lot of things like fighting and bullying and I just didn't know about that side of life and that's when the voices and doing impressions of school mates and teachers got me out of trouble, as it has with a lot of other people where humour has got them out of a jam.

When I was 16, I auditioned at RADA and out of 34 I got down to the last 4 and they called me in and said 'we really think you're ok and would do well here but you're 16. What we suggest you do is come back when you're 18' but by then I'd seen a documentary about actors without Equity cards and how much they struggled and how actors who come out of RADA with an Equity card are straight into work, so I thought the quickest way to get an Equity card was to do stand-up, so I did that and entered a competition called The Pub Entertainer of the Year Award with my partner Josh Walker and we ended up winning it and we got a lot of gigs off the back of it, so we got our Equity card and we were earning money. I didn't have any parental financial support so the thought of going back to school and being broke when I was earning and performing seemed silly. In hindsight I wished I had gone back but I couldn't afford to, so stand up was my bag, which I did for about 5 years. My partner decided to play golf in South Africa so I tried it on my own for a bit and I hated it because when it goes well you've got a mate to share it with and when it didn't go well you had someone to console you and looking to yourself all the time is horrible so I ended up getting a day job working in this publishing company but I still did the odd voice over and now, that's more or less what I still do.

I was about 21 or 22 when I did 'Terrahawks' and it was one of these coincidences as to how I got the job. I was working for a Dutch publishing company called VNU selling advertising space but I also did voiceovers whenever I could, which was fairly infrequent, but I put together a telephone answer tape of celebrities answering your phone, different, wacky celebrities like John Wayne and Miss Piggy having an assignation of some kind and I got interviewed on the Graham Dene Show on Capital Radio Breakfast show, it was just a 3 minute thing but Gerry Anderson happened to be driving to work to concentrate on casting the Terrahawks and he heard me and as an

CALL SIGNS

One-Zero	Top Secret
Ten-Zero	Negative
Ten-Ten	Affirmative
Ten-Twenty	Location
Ten-Thirty	Standing by
Ten-Fourty	Battle Stations
Ten-Fifty	Launch
Ten-Ninety	Mayday

impressionist I could do a few voices, so he phoned Capital Radio and said 'that guy you interviewed, can I have his number?' which they gave to him, he phone me that evening and said 'Hello, I heard you on the radio, my name's Gerry Anderson' and I'm a massive of Captain Scarlett and Thunderbirds, so I thought it wasn't really him and made verbal gestures accordingly, but it was him and he invited me down to Bray Studios to audition. I went there and saw the puppets and he talked me through what he thought they should be like. Tiger Ninestein was head of the 'Terrahawks' and his puppet looked like Humphrey Bogart – without hair, so he said he was thinking of something like Humphrey Bogart, so I did the voice but he didn't think it worked. He then asked me who my favourite impression was at the moment and I said I'm winning points with Jack Nicholson, so he said to do Jack Nicholson. He said he loved the voice but it was too laid back so I just strengthened it up and got the role. He then told me about Leitenant Hero 'He's half Japanese and half American, this is his background, what do you think?' so I came up with a voice and that's how it happened, so I got Hero, Hawkeye and Ninestein as mainstay characters.

When it came to recording the Terrahawks episodes Ann Ridler, who played various character in it, would pick me up in her little MG Midget and we'd rattle down the M4 to Bray Studios, we'd be given two scripts and the four of us would sit round a table and read through them. If any new characters came up Gerry would ask us if we had any ideas and we'd try various things until he was happy with it, then we'd have a lunch break and Windsor Davies and I would go to the pub and have a couple of pints of what they call 'wife beater' or Stella Artois then we'd come back and record them. We recorded two episodes a day, but it was only for one day a month. We'd all sit round a table which was divided into four, each with a mic, and it was pretty easy. If someone fluffed you could just do it again. I ended up doing about 15 characters and we did 39 episodes in total and it was great fun.

One of Ninestein's more memorable lines he used to say a lot to Mary Falconer was 'you're a day at the beach' I don't know whether he meant anything by that, and I did enjoy saying 'Terrahawks, stay on this channel, this is an emergency' it was a great line to kick the whole programme off with.

We didn't see the episodes being made because it's a time consuming process and we'd have just got in the way but we did have drinks with the puppeteers and we saw some of the models that came out after they'd been blown up. As a voice artist, the great thing was that they did the voices first so there was none of this lip synching which is quite hard work plus it allows you to have more freedom to come up with something and there would be greater restrictions in terms of the script if you need to make changes if it doesn't always 'speak' well.

In the revamped version of Captain Scarlett I played Captain Magenta (not quite Scarlett) and played some other incidental characters. In Thunderbirds, for example, you might recognise an actors voice for another character and think, that's the guy who's playing Scott Tracey, whereas because the new Captain Scarlett was the most expensive animation ever made in Britain at the time, I think it still is, Gerry wanted new baddies and different voices that aren't identifiable which was a good idea so I was brought in to basically do the baddies and I played lots of them. I actually phoned him up once I got wind of the show and said 'Hello, remember me?' and he said 'Oh alright, come on up' and he sat me down and said 'I want you because you're an impressionist and want you to come in and be the incidental baddies' and we decided whether they're going to be South African or Dutch, or whatever it was going to be, on the day to separate them as my vocal tones wouldn't be registered by the viewers as anyone of the main characters, so for me it was great. It meant I could show off, basically.

I had quite a specific brief for Captain Magenta. They had three directors for the programme and one of them, David Lane, called me when I was on a beach in Sardinia with my family and wanted to talk about Captain Magenta. He said to me to "Get out 'Good Fellas' and watch Ray Liota" and he would open up by saying "I always wanted to be a gangster" so I watched that film and just thought I'll do something of that ilk, so Magenta was a sleazy, womanising "Hey, I want to get inside your pants" kind of character. In fact, I would say that it's probably THE most specific brief I've ever had, which is great because it gave me something to work on. I get so many scripts now for commercials and documentaries where the producer sits down and asks 'here's the script, what do you think?' well, where can I start? This could go from Donald Duck to Ronald Reagan, so it's actually quite nice to have a brief.

I worked on a few scenes with Ben Stevens (Captain Blue) who I worked with on Terrahawks and we're good mates and we've stayed in touch ever since then, in fact he stays at my house when he travels up to Scotland.

I do remember one storyline in particular which was deep and meaningful, which wasn't really aimed at kids just aimed at me who used to love the original Captain Scarlett and would like to revisit it which was about a probe that crashed to Earth at the North Pole and it was identified as a probe that had gone missing 15 years ago with all hands presumed dead, so Scarlett goes off in his jet to check it out when it crashes, everybody is dead apart from one person who's only just alive and has been infected by the Mysterons and it's actually Leitenant Green's dad, who is then relieved of her post so she could go and see her dad who she had presumed was dead and they're reunited and it's terribly emotional but then, of course, he's a Mysteron so he's trying to infiltrate and cause chaos and destruction to Spectrum and she ends up having to kill him and it was just very very emotional, we were all crying like a couple of wet blankets when we did it but it was really wonderful and I was thinking that it's a bit heavy for kids but it was a good show. Pity it bombed.

It wasn't particularly well paid if I'm honest with you but one thing in particular that was amazing and got us, as voice over artists, excited was that Gerry always made a lot of Americanisms in his shows because he wanted to sell it to America because that's where the big dough is and if it goes to America you'd get 150% of your original recording fee per episode, per station so every time they would motivate us and say 'it's gone on 7 stations in America... it's gone on 9 stations... it's gone on 22 stations...' and we were going "£40 x 150 x 39 episodes x 22..." the number were getting vast and eventually they turned

Jeremy Hitchen - a legend of Kids TV

around and said "Great, it's been sold to NBC" which was fantastic, BUT it meant a repeat value of ONE because it was networked and syndicated throughout America, so we didn't really cash in on that at all! I don't think any voice over artists do it for the money, you do it for the craic, it's good fun with good people.

I met my wife when I was working for VNU Business Publications and we ended up running the Personal Computer World show at Earls Court and we then started up our own business. I was still doing voiceovers but it's not a 9-5 job, you could have three gigs one week and then nothing for a month, so we started up a publishing and exhibition company and that was great. We had four beautiful children but we didn't see a great deal of them because we were working so much, so we ended up selling it and went to live in Spain. I was in a restaurant one evening ordering a Gin & Tonic standing next to some chap who was putting a radio station together and he said 'You sound like you could present on radio' and I said 'well, that's my bag really' so I ended up doing a breakfast show on a station called Spectrum FM and did that for a couple of years, then got poached by another station and so on. After about 4 years in Spain, which was brilliant and had a lovely time, it was time to bring the kids back to a bit of reality from Marbella and that's when I moved to Edinburgh where I do voice overs there and I'm quite busy because I can do impressions and 3 or 4 characters at a time but they only have to pay me once, but that's fine.

Then my wife said she wanted to start a magazine, so we did that. The first one was called 'Spain' and we launched another called 'Living Abroad' and funnily enough my wife, my daughters and I are all into the Edinburgh Festival which is a fantastic festival of all sorts of things and we tried to get information on it but the information we got was rubbish. The Fringe guide was just dates and venues and times, it didn't actually tell you anything, it can't do because people pay to be part of the Fringe, so they can't produce a magazine that says this is shit or this is great, so my wife said there should be a magazine that brings all the Festivals – The International, the Fringe, the music festival, the book festival and so on – together that's a 'best of' so we launched 'Edinburgh Festivals Magazine' which does unbelievably well, it's a beautiful magazine and we love working on it, readers love it, advertisers love it. About 6 years ago my wife, who doesn't cook (I do the cooking) said to me how Scotland is such a magnificent place for food, it's beef is wonderful, it has game and fish and it's got it all going on – little haggises running out in the fields – so she suggested we create a food festival that's part of the Edinburgh festival so we launched 'Foodies at the Festival' and it was mobbed. It was an outdoor event that is a celebration of food, drinks and food masterclasses, chefs demonstrations from top chefs and it was great, so then we launched one at Hampton Court Palace because I used to live round the corner and a little local knowledge always helps.

When you run an event in Olympia or the NEC, you don't have to worry about security or the weather, or water and waste and toilets, but when you put it in a field you have to make provisions for those sort of things so it's much harder work but there's something about being outdoors that's like a pressure cooker, you take the lid off and people relax.

2012 is our fourth year at Hampton Court Palace and what can I say? In the first hour today we had 5,000 people through the gates, we have sponsors like Scottish Power and BMW and over the three days we'll probably see between 40-45,000 people over the three days. People who are really passionate about food.

Jeremy Hitchen

To find out more about the Foodies Festival go to www.foodiesfestival.com where there is a full list of events planned for 2013 or follow them on Twitter @foodiesfestival

SARAH JANE HONEYWELL
HIGGLEDY HOUSE, MIGHTY MITES, TIKKABILLA, CBEEBIES

Cbeebies fun-sized pocket rocket, Sarah Jane is a familiar face on Tikkabilla, Mighty Mites and inside Higgledy House and would brighten the day of many a child - and quite a few dads too! This self confessed animal loving, acrobatic, vegan punk hasn't been afraid to stir up a bit of controversy to highlight a worthy cause. Plus, she supports Bristol City FC. What a trooper!

I first got the bug for performing when I was 2 years old. My sister was at a dance class and I just joined in... I used to watch old musical films with my grandma all the time too. I didn't really receive any advice about presenting for children but what I would say is just have fun, if you're having fun hopefully the kids will too.

Sarah Jane Honeywell

I just love to work.... working is my life and as it's so hard to get work in this industry, when I do I cherish it and give it my all... there are no days off, no holidays, no sick pay and no pension but I love it. Ideally I'd love to either present an animal show or be the lead in a horror movie or in a comedy show.

Children's TV isn't all what it seems on screen. I have a filthy sense of humour and there's a lot of adult jokes on set.... most of us are in our 30's so if we were really like our screen personas I think that would be more of a worry than the fact that our humour can be a bit base.

In 2011 I took part in a photoshoot that some thought was a bit daring for a children's TV presenter and there was a bit of a backlash from that. I was dropped from Cbeebies.... however I think it was well received and apart from the odd mum having a go at me I think most people thought it was about time.

Also that year I posed topless on a plate in Trafalgar Square to highlight World Vegan Day. The People for the Ethical Treatment of Animals (PETA) had organised a 'Relate to what's on your plate' campaign and they asked me because I had used some of their footage for my Karma video. I thought it was a great idea.... it was embarrassing though and I did feel very vulnerable.

As part of my other work I've appeared in the musical 'Cats' and as an animal lover it felt amazing to play one of them. I loved being in that show. I've loved all of my career so far and as for work in the future I'd love to be the Doctors new assistant.... or play Roxy in 'Chicago'.... or do 'Dancing On Ice'.

When I'm not working I like to read a lot, I watch a lot of horror ..... I do have a dark side and I'm not afraid of that but I also like fluffy things... one of my close friends described me as a dichotomy. I'm also a big fan of Bristol City FC. My partner is a life long City fan... he took me there about 10 years ago and I fell in love with the club and once I'm in love that's it!

Sarah Jane Honeywell

You can read more about Sarah Jane on her website www.sarah-jane.biz

WAYNE JACKMAN

PLAY SCHOOL, RADIO ROO, TIMMY TIME, ROARY THE RACING CAR,
BALAMORY, BODGER & BADGER, TWEENIES, BLUE PETER, BASIL BRUSH...

You may know Wayne primarily for his stints presenting Play School, Radio Roo and playing Jiffy in Gigglish Allsorts but his involvement in kids TV goes way beyond that, writing over 2,500 scripts for TV and radio, and winning several awards along the way - a list of credits longer than Humpty's food shopping list!

I was a late starter in catching the 'acting bug', much preferring football and art up until my mid-teens. That said I had always had a keen interest in magic tricks and spent a lot of my pocket money and cash earned from odd jobs on new magic apparatus. I must have bored my parents stiff with endless fumbling attempts at sleight of hand but with practice I eventually grew confident enough to start performing at children's birthday parties - actually earning money! I still have my first 'business card' with the slogan 'Hey Presto, it's Wayne Jackman' - although listing ventriloquism as one of my talents may have been pushing it!

In my final two years at Grammar school I was given parts in the school plays and realised with a thrill that people actually laughed at my antics. Nevertheless, I continued on the art path and went off to the local Art College. Here, I spent many lunchtimes in the library endlessly watching a video documentary about James Dean. My head was starting to turn although I then gained a place at Trent Poly Photographic College. I didn't last long behind the camera and every spare moment was spent at the local Am Dram society. Soon I was learning speeches and auditioning for London Drama Schools. I won a place at the Central School and even persuaded my long-suffering local education authority to give me a full grant! (Those were the days!) Off I trolled to learn to do up my flies and not bump into the furniture

The World Cup-winning England side of 1966 was a big influence and football was my goal. I might even have signed on schoolboy terms with Brighton & Hove Albion but art was too big a pull. I hung up my boots and picked up my paintbrush. With that in mind, dear old Tony Hart was an influence with his fantastic art programmes and I was lucky enough to write for him in later years. Other than that, the 'Blue Peter' presenters were big in those days as were TV programmes such as 'Wacky Races'. Later the aforementioned James Dean became my god and heavily influenced my decision to try out as an actor. Becoming a 'Play School' presenter later might seem far removed from the iconic red jacket and white tee shirt but I did buy a motorbike for a time.

After leaving Central I appeared in a lot of fringe theatre shows and also did a stint on BBC Radio's rep company. An early TV role was in a play called 'The White Guard' along with Martin Clunes. I then heard through a friend that Play School was one of the most lucrative engagements on BBC TV at the time - not because the fees were high but because you often got to record five shows in a week. Five shows, five fees!

Apart from the dosh it seemed to me that as a presenter you got to do so many different things and express many sides of whatever talent you may have had - acting, singing, dancing, painting, presenting, story-telling, puppetry, talking to stuffed toys! I reckoned I might be able to do that and so simply wrote in to ask for an audition. As luck would have it, the BBC were revamping the show at the time and were indeed on the look-out for new presenters. I was summoned to North Acton rehearsal rooms and in front of a panel of producers and execs pulled out my magic tricks, sang the Grand Old Duke of York and performed a Japanese tea ceremony in cod Japanese along with my old teddy from childhood. It seemed to go well enough for them to ask me back for a further audition the following week. After that I was plonked in a real TV studio and asked to undergo a camera test. That was scary! However, good or bad, they seemed to recognise some glimmer of ability and I was signed up for my first batch of shows. My very first appearance was with another newcomer, Liz Watts and two stalwarts, Ben Thomas and Elizabeth Millbank.

The most troublesome toy was Hamble. Her head kept falling off! Many a take was ruined at the last moment by Hamble falling sideways as if drunk and losing her head, literally. Being an old vinyl doll from the 60s she was impossible to replace since finding an identical doll was a very long shot. And so the production crew were stuck with her. She was also pretty grubby through wear and tear and I recall once sitting next to her in the make-up room as we were both given a foundation base and powdered. Big Ted and Little Ted were also unique but much less bother. They were both hardened professionals and a joy to work with. You could also jam their arms and legs into position so they didn't fall over. Humpty and Jemima were also greatly loved by the crew and audience but not quite as revered since there were at least three of each of them. Being soft toys they were easier to replicate and the best ones were kept purely for studio recordings whilst their stand-ins were used in rehearsals. They were also the only toys allowed out of the building since we had duplicates. Often 'Play School' presenters were asked to open school fetes and either stand-in Humpty or Jemima would accompany them. On occasions I used to arrive with Humpty belted up next to me on the car passenger seat. And he never got travel sick. What a guy.

The history of 'Gigglish Allsorts' is an interesting one. Originally the show was simply called 'Allsorts' and ran weekly for many years at lunchtimes on ITV. At that time all the various ITV companies bid for slots and so each of the five weekdays were filled with five different shows, often from different regions (ie: Thames, Granada, Central etc). 'Competing' shows included 'The Riddlers', 'Let's Pretend' and, of course, 'Rainbow' (which I was chuffed to write for later. Zippy is a legend!)

Later, the slot changed to around 3.30pm - tea time TV. I can't quite recall the timings but I think we were at one time told that Allsorts would not be returning that season although the repeats ensured that it was still on screen. Perhaps

Wayne as Jiffy

there was another show that took the slot, it's a while ago and hard to remember. However, soon the call came through that we were 'back'! I think I took the call on a train to Wales on one of the very early mobile phones. The signal was bad, especially as Wales has quite a lot of sidings and tunnels. I was on my way to join up with fellow cast members, Bonzo, JJ and Box since we were in the middle of an Allsorts theatre tour at the time. Naturally my fellow cast members were delighted at the news and the theatre shows that day had an extra 'zing'. The show was revamped and took the name 'Gigglish Allsorts' with a new theme tune. And so, off we all went back to Manchester for another block of a month or so of rehearsals and recordings and yet more fun and games ensued.

Had the show not returned it would have been disappointing but all the cast had many other irons in the fire and other TV jobs to pursue. Jane Cox (JJ) has of course made a big success of her role in 'Emmerdale', Andrew Wightman (Bonzo) is a big-time TV producer and Julie Westwood (Box) was/is a puppeteer on the enormously popular 'Lazy Town'. Since 'Allsorts' I have mostly written children's TV shows but still occasionally manage to wangle myself a role in my scripts such as 'Balamory'.

Jiffy the character is doing rather well for himself nowadays. After the 'Gigglish Allsorts' house was demolished to make way for a Starbucks, Jiffy initially proved a little cantankerous. He refused to leave, creating for himself a tent out of his over-sized jacket and installing himself in the corner of the building site whilst the works continued around him. The Starbucks management offered him a laptop by way of a bribe to scarper, which he soon mastered. However, once Jiffy realised that the new Starbucks offered free Wi-Fi he stayed on, settling himself into the window table. Before too long he was inventing games on his computer which fellow customers were keen to play. One thing led to another and Jiffy now has a penthouse office at Apple's Californian HQ. Steve Jobs may have been the face of Apple but Jiffy was the brains. Currently Jiffy is developing a baseball cap with inbuilt mobile phone, games console and computer tablet that also plays marbles.

What I do recall from those times are the various scrapes and injuries I suffered - the time when the cockatoo on 'Play School' bit my ear and wouldn't let go until lovely Wendy Duggan, the animal wrangler, stepped in; JJ on 'Allsorts' opening the shed door and smashing me on the head causing me to 'be a trooper' and finish the scene pulling down my baseball cap to hide the blood flowing down; jumping out of a canoe on 'Radio Roo' on a pond in South London and slicing my foot on glass requiring a hospital visit and a tetanus jab.

But of course I have other funny memories. Carol Chell on 'Play School' pretending to be a table with spilled sticky jam running down her table leg was a hoot. As a writer I attended some 'Rainbow' filming and remember conversing with Bungle, only to be told the actor wasn't actually inside the skin but was on a coffee break. I had a small role in one of my scripts for 'Balamory' which required me to step into a pre-arranged cab - only to be beaten to it by a member of the public who asked to taken to taken home. And the cab drove off!

As I earlier mentioned, I anticipated being the new James Dean once I left drama school. I was moody, I was a loner, I could scowl with the best of them. The only thing I didn't have was an agent versed in the wiles of Hollywood. So, it was fringe theatre for me. But that was fantastic experience. From humble beginnings as an ASM in lunchtime pub theatre in Brighton I eventually progressed to a show upstairs at the Old Red Lion in Islington, London where the whole cast of nine had to change whilst squashed in the gents' toilet. Given that I started the first scene in that show stark naked it was an interesting time for all.

So, it wasn't a conscious decision but rather an opportunity to showcase my various skills and get a foot on the ladder. Since then Children's TV has largely become what I do. Maybe we were made for each other? I still sometimes hanker after other things and maybe they will come about. But I wouldn't change a moment of my time thus far in Children's TV - it's such fun!

The best way to get writing done is to have a contract, a demanding producer and an overdraft. I avoid distractions by locking myself away with absolutely no music, family, radio, TV or, preferably, road-works outside. Silence, silence, silence. I like to 'hear' my characters speak and often act them out myself.

I also have a note stuck to my computer, which I have found very useful. It reads 'Don't get it right, get it written.' I mean that you should just write - anything. A page of disjointed, half-baked waffle is more encouraging than a blank page. The act of writing/typing will engage your creative juices and lead who-knows-where?

At the start of his working day the artist Paul Klee spoke of 'letting his pencil take a walk'. Exactly! Let your fingers take a walk around the keyboard (or your pen around the paper). Even write an email. Just get started.

The best thing about writing for children is being able to be a child again myself. And knowing that whatever character I am creating it will hopefully amuse or inform a whole new generation of children. I feel a responsibility to my audience but not in a dry way. Imagination is king. It's what will engage and encourage the audience. And who knows - maybe something I have written will stay with a child for a long time, maybe just as a fond memory but possibly as a way of thinking in a small way.

A show I wrote for the BBC in the 80s called 'Radio Roo' is probably my favourite comedy work. For a start I got to play Dennis, one of the two main characters (the other was Clive - a kangaroo!) It was aimed at a slightly above pre-school age range and was pure, out and out comedy. No message, no education, just laughs. The set-up was that I ran a pirate radio station with Clive, constantly at odds with the local killjoy on the Council. We had guest characters in each episode ranging from a lady wrestler to a trumpet-playing escaped convict. It was so freeing to write and such fun to film, both in studio and on location. And the production team were largely the same as from my 'Play School' days and so it was 'all friends together'. Hopefully it was popular with the audience too. Even this week an estate agent I had dealings with couldn't help but mention it as a show he had watched as a child. Either I'm very old or estate agents are getting younger!

More recently, my favourite character to write for has been Aardman's pre-school Timmy from 'Timmy Time'. Timmy is a little lamb and the show was spun off from the slightly older-skewing, 'Shaun The Sheep' which was itself a spin-off from 'Wallace & Grommit'. 'Timmy Time' is without dialogue, apart from the various animal 'noises' and so proved to be a little tricky to write for since everything had to be visual, without any verbal explanations as to why characters were doing what they were doing. For this reason it really honed down the narrative to pure, simple, emotion and intention. Universal. The producer, Jackie Cockle, was kind enough to say once that I seemed to 'live' Timmy. I appreciated that and it's true. I miss him and hope he'll come back one day.

Dennis and Clive from Radio Roo

When the first of my scripts was nominated for an award I was naturally delighted but, quite honestly, didn't give it a great deal of thought. Any show that is recognised is totally a team effort and other contributors to the series ought to feel equally acknowledged. We all do our jobs and the bonus is that your peers and the audience can appreciate your team effort.

Awards ceremonies are exciting but also daunting. For some you have to dress up posh and the bow tie can be a nuisance. It can also be all too easy to imbibe too much through nerves at being among so many exalted strangers! Nevertheless it's pleasing to have something to bung on the office shelf should you be so lucky as to win something. It doesn't make your next script any better mind you - nor, necessarily do the offers come flooding in. Graft away and take pleasure in a good job done.

As for other roles, having done a few pantos in my time then I have to say playing Dick Whittington at the Connaught, Worthing was a highlight of the genre. The lovely, gracious, Hugh Lloyd played Alderman Fitzwarren and Sophie Warren, a brilliantly talented actor and singer who died tragically young, was Alice. God bless them both. It was an extremely well-written production in which I also had a chance to 'act' as well as playing the fool. It was dramatic as well as slapstick. "Oh no it wasn't!"

Other theatre roles which stand out in my memory are Romeo (Romeo & Juliet), Bottom (Midsummer Night's Dream), Stanley (The Birthday Party), Mr Sloane (Entertaining Mr Sloane) and George in the Young Vic's production of the Beatles musical, John, Paul, George, Ringo & Bert. Maybe my three years at Central weren't wasted after all.

I mentioned before that imagination is key to writing for children - it is in any writing although with older audiences 'real life and truth' perhaps impinge more, certainly in soaps. That's not to say that writing for children - I'm talking about younger children here - shouldn't address real life issues, it can and ought to, but in a heightened, 'simplified' way. Too many complex issues can cloud the watching/reading experience. A strong narrative with a related minor plot, which is all resolved at the end is, in my opinion, essential. Children want and need resolution but also some fun and entertainment along the way. Story, story, story.

I have at times attempted to write adult sit-coms or drama scenarios which get so far but then falter because I want to introduce a dragon or a talking toaster. I'm not sure if this is a good thing or a bad thing. Put it this way, I'm not yet a scriptwriter for Eastenders - unless they have an opening for a talking toaster?

I tend not to dwell too much on the politics and machinations of those 'high-ups' in Children's TV who make decisions. No doubt they are often, quite naturally, motivated by questions of marketing, scheduling, profit and viewing figures. It's the real world. That said, in my second-hand experience, 'the bosses' do genuinely seem to care about Children's TV, certainly here in the UK. However, there now seems to be a trend for longer runs of 'solid' proposals - those series that can guarantee an audience and ease of marketing. Gone are the days when a readily accessible department head would 'find 5 minutes' to listen to your idea, like it and authorise a 13 part 'test run' on that basis. Nowadays, through limited finance and so many more competitors, that call, that risk, is a non-starter. I wonder if we would now have the library and characters of Bagpuss, Roobarb, Zippy, Thomas, Postman Pat, Humpty...etc if it wasn't for the fact that various execs hadn't, in earlier days, just said 'yes' over a cup of tea?

To end on a positive note, I perceive that currently, the younger practitioners, those newer to the game, seem so full of energy and ideas that it all bodes well - if they are given the chance by the 'high-ups'. Bye now, I'm expecting Muffin The Mule for Tea and Hay.

Wayne Jackman

You can read more about Wayne's career at www.waynejackman.com

2 CHRIS JARVIS
PLAYDAYS, FULLY BOOKED, SHOW ME SHOW ME, CBBC, CBEEBIES

One of the original Cbeebies presenters, Chris has carved himself a successful career in children's TV, whether it's in continuity, reading out birthday greetings or stints in the broom cupboard. Together with fellow legend Pui Fan Lee, they have created the popular "Show Me Show Me" and a new show for one of the 'daddy legends'. Chris was also known for lurking around the broom cupboard as The Anorak. I know!!!

The legends of my childhood are without doubt the greats of Children's TV: Brian Cant, Derek Griffiths - who I've done 2 pantos with, the casts of 'Rentaghost' and 'Worzel Gummidge'. As well as all the great voice artists and impressionists like Faith and Janet Brown, Mike Yarwood, Kenny Everett and Dick Emery. My true heroes were of course my family - not just my parents but entertaining aunts and uncles.

I have always been a performer at school and in drama groups, I cannot remember a time when I haven't enjoyed entertaining and therefore I cannot remember when I first started yearning for a career in show business.

I have worked at Butlin's many times but not wearing a red coat... something I would have loved! My plans were to audition to be a redcoat but I landed a great job in radio which took all my time. When I was 18 I used to host a lunchtime kids show on Radio Orwell and Saxon Radio in Suffolk - I'm not sure what the good people up there had done wrong, but the show lasted two hours every Saturday and took most of my time to prepare and write sketches for.

I remember feeling very uncomfortable on my first TV appearance! It took ages before I could relax and years before I got the chance to be myself. What I do now is pretty much me! I first worked with Pui when CBeebies started in 2002... we met on the first day & immediately clicked. We share a sense of humour and a love of Radio 4.

When working with very young children, animals, precarious props etc.... mishaps & script deviations are commonplace. There have been many puddles on the studio floor and unspeakable smells but the most memorable mis-adventure in the 90s ended up on 'Auntie's Bloomers' and shown many times; I was dressed as a superhero and had to rescue a granny. In this case, the old lady was in fact a mannequin that hadn't been fully dressed. When I lifted her over my shoulder, the camera got more than a flash of plastic. We had a fabulous floor manager called Tom who had the most infectious and loud laugh who kept us giggling about it all day.

There were loads of guests I worked with that made me star struck. All the big super groups, pop stars and celebrities most people would love to meet but a few of my own personal heroes include: Nick Park, Bernard Cribbins, Su Pollard, Stephen Fry, JK Rowling, the Divine Comedy, Graham Fellows.... it was an utter joy to meet them and discover how genuine they are.

The Anorak was a term created by Andy Archer - a DJ on Radio Caroline in the 1960s - to describe the overenthusiastic fans who used to paddle out to the ship in dinghys. He was also my producer on the radio and suggested the character... so he was audio before video.

I'm not sure how he ended up in the Broom Cupboard - security was rather lax in those days before tags, fobs and ID cards. These days, unable to break into broadcast centres, he has switched his attention to aeroplane spotting. He and Norma are living in their camper-van in the long stay car park of Terminal 5 at Heathrow. The fee to leave the car park is now so huge it would be cheaper to buy a new van. Efforts to evict them proved futile.

I've worked with the likes of Nick Wilton, Derek Griffiths and Bernard Cribbins in panto and all are sensational people and great teachers. I remember standing

Chris & Pui

in the wings of Richmond theatre watching Bernard doing his opening spot - I never missed a show.

Nick is unique and hilarious - such a wonderful character artist and deserves a massive break in a sitcom. Derek is also extremely talented and funny. I remember Bernard Cribbins doing his Uncle Bulgaria voice on the backstage tannoy.... how cool was that?! Pui and I came up with a TV show for Bernard - it's being filmed right now for Cbeebies! {Uncle Jack's Boat}

I'm most proud of 'Show Me Show Me' - I can remember where I was when Pui and I hit upon that name and idea. It was developed by the most incredibly talented people and we're lucky that it's still going strong. We're co-writing series 4 which started filming in November this year {2012}.

Myself and Pui have our own stage show which brings together all our party pieces - the songs, characters, sketches... in fact anything from TV that works on stage as well as sections written especially for theatre. Little Bo Peep, Humpty and the gang all drop in to say hello! We absolutely love touring the UK and meeting the audience; it's a joy to be invited back to so many fantastic cities and towns.

Chris Jarvis

You can keep up to date with Chris and Pui's latest projects and their tour dates on their website www.chrisandpui.com

PAUL KASEY

DOCTOR WHO, THE SARAH JANE ADVENTURES

From the West End stage to invading the Earth and appearing at the Olympics. Not many people can boast that on their CV, but Paul Kasey can. He's also responsible for a new generation of children cowering behind the sofa as the man behind the masks of the The Cyber Leader, The Judoon Captain, a Clockwork Droid and an Auton, to name but a few. Paul takes a look back on the events that ultimately altered his career path.

I was born in Leicestershire where I was brought up on a 310 acre farm where my father was the farm manager and my mother was a nurse. I was the third child with three other siblings, one brother and two sisters. We lived a very typical country life where most weekends were spent either helping out on the farm or taking our horses to a horse show or event. We were all very lucky to have our own horses and as anyone who has ever had a horse knows they take up a lot of your spare time.

My older brother was very much following in my father's footsteps helping on the farm and learning all the farm crafts whilst studying at an agricultural college. My older sister wanted to be a hairdresser and also went to college to study. My younger sister was mad on horses and wanted to become a professional groom at a stable of which she did, and then there was me who ended up leaving home and Leicestershire to do something quite different in the end!

The farm was situated in the middle of nowhere with the local shops being about three miles away so you could say my upbringing was quite isolated in more ways than one, especially when there had been a bad winter and we had ten foot snow drifts outside our back door. On rare occasions we did have school friends come and stay, who loved the fact that we were surrounded by fields and lots of open space with all different types of animals, and that was basically my childhood.

At first like most teenagers when asked I was a little unsure of what I wanted to do, I was probably thinking I would follow in the footsteps of my mother and train to be a nurse, but there was a series of events that happened when I was eleven that changed my journey in life for good. My parents announced that they were going to divorce and decided that my older sister and brother were going to stay on the farm with my father, and my younger sister and I were going to live with my mother. It was not until a few years later I think, I must have been about fourteen and still at school when one day we had a leaflet through the door saying there was a local dance school opening that September. They were holding an open day for people to go and view and sign up. I'd always been a little theatrical and had what you might call an artistic flare for the arts but had never had an opportunity to pursue it! I have great memories of living on the farm but you lead a certain lifestyle and everything else seemed to me to be a million miles away until now. I persuaded my mum to take me to the open day to see what it was all about, my mum agreed to let me start having dance lessons that September. I was the only boy to start and at fourteen and a half years old I was quite late to start dancing but it was not long until I was living and breathing it. Looking back, I would spend every night at the weekend glued in front of the TV watching all the programs that had dancers in them as back then a lot of TV shows had dancers in them; such as Hot Gossip in the Kenny Everett show. I would drag my younger sister in to what was known as our best room which had a record player in it and would try to recreate some of the sequences that I had seen on the TV the night before.

My dance teacher's name was Sarah Jane Tindle and had been a professional dancer in London for many years. She then decided to move back to where her parents lived to open up a dance school. She'd been a Bluebell girl and had danced on a lot of TV shows over the years including the Morecambe & Wise show. One day she happened to mention to my mother that I should consider going away and training professionally, at the time the best place for boys to train was a place called Laine Theatre Arts in Epsom, Surry. My mother thought I was too young to venture away from home at sixteen and suggested that I stayed on at school for an extra year and take four more GCSE's, she was very adamant that no matter what career path I took I should have a good education behind me. So I did just that and with all my other spare time I would dance as it was in my blood and all I wanted to do.

That year I auditioned for the local pantomime of which I got a part performing in the chorus, as my dance teacher thought it would be a great experience for me. Prior to this I had received and sent off all the forms to audition for Laines. Whilst I was in rehearsal for the pantomime I had received a letter back saying they'd like to audition me in the February, but unfortunately I had a pantomime performance on the same day and they would not let me have the evening off. So I just had to make sure I was back in time for the half hour call, of which I just made it with seconds to go!

I finished the successful pantomime season and was back at school, when one day I walked in home to find my mother stood at the kitchen table and on it was a letter addressed to me. I knew exactly what it was and my heart jumped into my mouth. It was the letter I had been waiting for, the letter from Laines regarding my audition. I sat down and was scared to open it, my mother reassured me by saying "don't worry if they have not accepted you this year you can always audition again next year" I opened the letter and it said they would like to offer me a place in September. I was over the moon that I had been accepted and couldn't stop smiling for weeks.

My mother, like most mothers phoned everyone to let them know the good news. The year was 1990 and I turned 17, I remember it as though it was only yesterday. It was all systems go that summer with lots of forms to be filled out and a lot of organising to be done. Eventually everything got sorted out and I started Laine Theatre Arts that September. My mother took me down to where I was going to be living and sobbed all the way home apparently. I was very lucky in a way because my mother was very open minded and wanted all her children to have the opportunities to do what they wanted to do. I remember when she dropped me off, she said to me "It doesn't matter what happens I'm very proud of you, if you decide at some point it's not for you or you would prefer a different career and want to do something else, then that`s absolutely fine and you can come home."

My first year flew by and in your second year at Laines they allowed you to accept work whether that be pantomimes, summer seasons or the occasional trade show. A lot of very well known choreographers like Kim Gavin, who was at the time choreographing for Take That, along with Alan Harding who choreographed many of the children's and Royal Variety shows would come to Laines to audition for students to use. So from my second year onwards I started to do little bits of work and put them on to my CV. The course was for three years but I was offered a fourth year scholarship by Betty Laine to further my training, which I did. They were the best years of my life and I only have fond memories of my time at Laine Theatre Arts. I absolutely loved it and was like a sponge soaking up everything Betty Laine and her brilliant teaching faculty had to offer.

On leaving in 1994 I had lined up a summer season in Eastbourne to play one of the acromaniacs, who were a slap stick gymnastic troop. Once I had finished the season I started to audition for all the main dance agencies in London; Pineapple, Trends, Tommy Tucker, Success and Dancers of which I was successful in getting on their books. I ended up auditioning for all different types of work and musicals and one of the first jobs I was offered was a place in a ballet company, but I decided not to accept the 18 month contract as my preference was to do the more commercial work that was out there or maybe try to get into a west end musical.

Eventually after numerous auditions for many different musicals I landed my first West End Show. I was offered a chorus role in 'Grease' which was at the Dominion Theatre at the time; I ended up staying in the show for two years running. Once I'd finished that contract I went back to doing commercial work for a while until I auditioned for a brand new show that was coming over from Broadway call 'Fosse'. This was a tribute show to one of the world's greatest choreographers Bob Fosse. I must have had lady luck looking down on me that day as I was offered a part in the show and was back in the West End yet again for another year. Towards the end of my contract there was another series of events that came about that would eventually change my career direction for good, it would enable me to become the performer I am today. I had about three months to go in Fosse when I had a phone call from an agent saying that there were going to be auditions for Blade 2 and they were looking for strong physical performers to play the parts of the Reapers, of which they were casting for five parts and was I interested. How could I have said no! An opportunity like this does not come along that often in ones career. So I did the auditions and recalls and it then went quite. Like with most things, I would not hold my breath and put it to the back of my mind as I knew they were auditioning lots of people for the roles and with big jobs like this one, you never think you're in with a chance because of who you are up against. I hadn`t heard back from the film, my contract was coming to an end and I had been told that Fosse was going to be coming off the West End and going to go on either a European or world tour, with a fifteen week gap in between, would I be interested? As 'Fosse' was a dancer's dream job I could have carried on doing the show forever. It`s what most dancers hope for in their life time and was the perfect show to be in. Like many shows it required all the skills that you needed to be a West End performer: Dancing, singing and acting, in my case gymnastics. I said yes in principle and also got a job as a dancer/gymnast on a cruise ship for twelve weeks out of the fifteen weeks I was going to have free. It fitted in perfectly.

I still remember this day so vividly, it was a Wednesday I was in a queue at the bank on Regents Street of all places when my phone rang, it was my agent that I had auditioned for Blade 2 through. So I went outside to answer it, he said he had just got off the phone from the production company for the film and they would like to offer me one of the Reaper parts, filming in Prague for twelve weeks. He went on to tell me all the dates for the fittings, rehearsals and filming which I knew clashed with the tour and the cruise. I explained that both contracts were in the post so I would have to make a couple of phone calls to see if I could get out of them before I could accept the film. After doing a little celebratory dance and calling my mum I made the phone calls. Lucky for me they decided that because it was such a great opportunity they would not hold me to the contracts and would replace me on both jobs. I then quickly called the agent back to accept the film, Blade 2.

I received my twelve week filming contract for the film and the Special FX Company flew over from LA to do all the head and body casts for all the actors.

Over this period I think I ended up flying to and from Prague about six times. The film ended up extending for about three weeks and so did my contract. I had such a great time in Prague whilst working on Blade 2, and this was my first big introduction to prosthetics, playing creature roles, sitting in the make-up chair at some early hour of the morning, wearing contact lenses, eating very carefully at lunch time and drinking through a straw.

Once I had finished the film another agent of mine called Physicality, who specialised in all different types of physical performers with special skills contacted me about another film that was casting. I was lucky enough to have a meeting with Danny Boyle, the film was called '28 Days Later'.

I started to get offered filming days on the film as one of the featured infected. Prior to this my whole career had been mainly to do with dancing and singing, but I was soon to realise that there was a whole different genre of work out there playing roles that were movement based. This type of work had been unknown to me until now; I was slowly being introduced to a whole new world!

In between filming on these projects I would fill my diary the best I could with dancing work, lecturing and choreographing. A year or so after filming on '28 Days Later' I received a phone call about a casting that was going to be taking place for a new TV series. They were looking for performers who had got experience in prosthetics and movement. At that time there was no mention of what it was going to be called as I believe it was being kept very hush hush for the time being. I had already had a taster of this kind of work and had absolutely enjoyed the whole experience and process, so I jumped at the chance to audition. This is where I first met the one and only Ailsa Burk, who at the time was taking the castings for all the different roles that were going to be on offer. I was successful in my audition and was asked back to do a recall a couple of weeks later. This was going to be a workshop type recall with Ailsa, the director of the first block and the producers being present. The workshop lasted about three and a half hours in total, it was on a Friday and after the recall I was meeting up with a good friend of mine for a couple of drinks in Covent Garden as it was her birthday. Whilst we were sat there chatting away and catching up my phone rang, it was great news! I had been offered one of the roles on the new series of 'Doctor Who'. I couldn't believe it, I was so excited and could not wait to start filming.

Millennium FX was the company who were going to be making all the creatures, monsters and aliens for the show, so once again I had to have my head, body, hands and feet cast. We started to film the first block of which I played one of the Autons, and then went on to play various other roles in the first series of 'Doctor Who'. With what seemed to be the longest wait ever, the trailer and publicity for the first series of 'Doctor Who' was released. I could never have imagined the amazing reaction and excitement it created not only in the UK but worldwide. Once the series was aired, 'Doctor Who' was once again back in everybody's front rooms, scaring a whole new generation of people.

I was asked back to play a few different roles and work on the second series of 'Doctor Who'. Whilst filming I got to hear that there was going to be a spin-off show with John Barrowman in it. I had already met John on the first series of 'Doctor Who' where he played Captain Jack Harkness. Rumours had it that it was going to be a bit darker than Dr Who and was going to be aired after the water shed. Not that long after that I was approached and told about the new series and that there were going to be creatures in it. They asked if I would be interested in playing a role, the new series was called 'Torchwood' and the creature ended up being the Weevil. I played the Weevil for two series alongside the Blowfish, which first appeared in the opening sequence of the second series. Then came along 'The Sarah Jane Adventures' which was another spin off from 'Doctor Who' but this one was going to be a children's TV show. At times I would find myself filming on all three shows as the different productions would slightly overlap and I would flit from one show to another for a short period of time.

'Being Human' was the next production I was asked to be involved in and to play the part of Russel Tovey's werewolf. So you could say that's how it all came about, as you can see there was definitely a sequence of events that happened in my life that got me to where I am today. If I could turn back the clock I would and do it all over again!

I've now been working in the filming industry, bringing to life and playing different roles for about ten years. This has in one way or another taken up most of my time but when I get asked and can fit it in I still like to accept dance, lecturing and choreographic work. Once the scales started to tip and I started to get more character roles the dancing work took a back seat for a while. What I like about playing all these different roles is that they are very much movement based and can require just as much physical fitness as I had when I was doing all the dancing, gymnastic and contortion work. Having a background that has the understanding of movement and the physical knowledge has helped me tenfold with what I do now and the characters I play. My first choice now would definitely to play the characters I do, I'm very lucky to be able to say that I felt personally satisfied with all the work I had done and had trained for, prior to the direction change that happened with my career. I've also had the opportunity of being a movement director and advisor for other productions, rehearsing, advising and training actors for roles that require a specific and different type of movement.

I have been asked in the past what are the differences if any in the types of work that I have experienced. With training and being a professional dancer for many years your fitness level always stays at a high level and they sort of go hand in hand. Where with playing character roles, yes you do get fitter when playing them but you also have to maintain and have a high level of fitness to start with. Life as a dancer is challenging in many ways but playing character roles is constantly challenging in lots of other ways, there is never a moment that goes by that you are not 100% concentrating on the task ahead. When having body casts done for work it is best to make sure your physique does not change too much as this can be used on many different occasions over a long period of time. I've been lucky in this as my body weight, shape and size has not changed that much over the years. I like to eat healthy and keep fit but, if I feel that a certain role will be more physically demanding than usual I step up my fitness regime as required.

Like the majority of viewers, I too spend my Saturday night in watching Doctor Who with my family if I'm around and not working. I do remember watching Doctor Who as a child but it used to petrify me and give me nightmares, so my mum would stop me from watching it. Now, in bringing to life the monsters, creatures and aliens on the show I am very aware that with the great story lines, costumes, special effects, the way it is filmed and with the dramatic music score added. I now know why it scared the living daylights out of me as a child. I now thankfully do not spend as much time hiding behind the sofa with a cushion in front of me!

When I receive and read the scripts, whether it's one of Russell T. Davies or Steven Moffat's, you can feel the tension that there will end up being on the TV screen for the viewers. I do get an idea of how they might be filmed, the shots they might use in the final edit and how scary the episode is going to be when watched. But when I'm on set it can feel quite different from the end product that I end up watching as a lot of the effects are added on later. It's just as exciting for me to watch an episode as everybody else.

When I have my fittings for a role I do often get to see the designs and concepts first and quite often than not for me they tell you a lot about the character; how it is going to move and what type of mannerisms it might take on. It's always good to have this in mind and know what you're going to look like on the outside as being on the inside can be very different to what is being portrayed on the outside of the make-up. Also with most of the characters I've played they look scary enough in their design so I know that to bring them alive will not be hard, and a more subtle approach will be needed. Whereas with a select few I know that more movement will be required to enhance the scary factor of the character. This is obviously also down to what is required within the context of the scene and the storyline you are filming. For example the Weevil in 'Torchwood', the design of the creature already comes across as a nasty piece of work and evil. That combined with the fact that in the first scene I filmed, it was scripted that I would be ripping the throat out of the hospital porter. So from then on I had a good idea of how the weevil would react in most circumstances and the characteristics it might have, along with the type of scenes that might follow in the two series of Torchwood.

All the characters I have played and suits I have worn have come with completely different challenges in one way or another. The Judoon Captain's costume isn't that heavy at all but because of the amount of animatronics within his head it can make it quite heavy when picking it up. But the good thing is the way it had been made and put together because I wear a harness that holds piano wires that fit into the top of the head on the inside which takes the majority of the weight off me. Generally the more animatronics used to give the character facial expressions the heaver they can be. The Slitheens and Blathereens are probably the largest costume I have worn, if we were filming in small areas there was not much room for anyone else, with their big bodies, long arms and claws. Cybermen were different, as you had to take off your fibre glass cyber pants before you could sit down.

Generally I can walk down the street and not be recognised but that is dependent on where I am and what I'm doing. My friends, family and their friends all know what I do for a living now. I can go to the supermarket and no one is aware of what I do unless they know me. Now there are a lot of fans connected to the programmes that I have been a part of, so if I'm doing something that is somehow connected in any way then I am instantly recognised. I recently had the pleasure of working on the opening ceremony of the Olympics with lots of amazing volunteers. Whilst taking the auditions I would quite often get approached as they would recognise me, more from the behind the scenes footage and interviews that I had appeared in. Out of the thousands that auditioned a few of them were fans of my work. It was not long into the rehearsal period that the word got round and the questions came thick and fast.

When they make a cast of your body they use the same plaster cast as if you'd broken an arm or leg. The first time I had casts taken of my body was for Blade 2. I remember when I went to have mine done they were very good at explaining the process, what I might feel like at times and said if I was to ever feel anxious, panicky or claustrophobic, I was just to concentrate on my breathing, in through my nose and out through my mouth. Because the time had been taken to explain the process, and with being so well informed, I ended up really enjoying the whole experience. When I came to have all my casts done for 'Doctor Who' at

Millennium FX. I remember being sat in their casting room, waiting to start the whole process when I was asked if I had ever had this process done before and for what, my replay was yes and for Blade 2! The process was explained again to me which was good because quite a few years had passed since I had had my previous casts done, so it refreshed my memory in what to expect. There were a lot of technicians in the room at the time as time is the essence when doing a body cast because the plaster of Paris sets very quickly. They have to work together at such a fast pace, as a well organised team for this to go to plan. This process is a taster of what it is like wearing prosthetics, animatronics heads and suits. I'm not claustrophobic in any way but for someone who does have reservations about being trapped, stuck or glued into something for long periods of time then I would guess it's not for them. Playing these types of roles is not for everyone, but for me I LOVE IT! It doesn't bother me at all being in prosthetics all day. For example on Blade 2 I'd be in the make-up chair at about 5am in the morning as it took around 4 hours to complete the make-up application, go on to set and film for the whole morning, have lunch very carefully as to not damage any of the make-up, back to the make-up chair for any checks before I would film for the second part of the day until we wrapped. At the end of the day I would then go back to the make-up chair to have the make-up removed of which took up to 2 hours. I have to add at this point and as you may already know that not all the roles I have played are like this. Take for example the Cybermen; it would take two technicians about ½ an hour to get me into my suit and in-between camera set ups the head would be taken off, at lunch we would come out of the whole suit.

Quite often prosthetics are glued down around your eyes and mouth and the solution that they use to take them off with is oil based as it breaks down the glue. So when it comes to lunch time it is best not to eat anything too greasy like chips for example otherwise the glue would start to breakdown and the prosthetics would start to come unstuck. This would create a lot more work for the make-up artist to repair before the afternoons filming. I also find that eating small amounts at a time and in front of a mirror can also help not to damage the make-up in anyway. Lunchtime can sometimes be a slow process if you are taking extra care not to cause any mishaps!

It's hard to say which has been my favourite role and scene to date because I'd probably end up listing every role and scene I'd ever filmed, for all different types of reasons. One of the episodes that tends to stay in my mind is 'The Girl in the Fireplace' written by Stephen Moffat. I remember receiving the script which, when I read it, sent childhood chills down my back. I played the Clockwork droid and in the first scene where I appear, there is the young Madame De Pompadour sat on her bed with the Doctor by her side. The Doctor happens to look under her bed of which I'm there hiding keeping very still and waiting, then all of a sudden, with all my might, my hand reaches out to grab him. For me, as a child I always thought there was something hiding under my bed. So when I read the script and went on to film the episode I always had these memories of my childhood checking under the bed every night before I got into it, and how scared I used to be in the back of my mind. All this aside, I ended up loving the whole episode, the era it was set in, costumes and the story that was being told, it was just so wonderful to watch.

There's also the iconic baddie, Cybermen with their new look and design. When reading Russell's scripts and how they were going to be portrayed within the scenes: Strong, powerful, scary and eerie. It was such an exciting moment for me to be asked to play such an amazing iconic character.

Now I'm on a roll and all my memories are coming flooding back to me I feel there are two other characters and great moments I would have to mention at this point. The first one being when I read one of the opening scenes to the second series of 'Torchwood' and I was introduced to the sports car driving Blowfish. I thought to myself, wow this is going to be so cool to play. We filmed the scenes late at night so it was dark and all the streets were wetted down of which they used off duty firemen and their Fire engine to do this. I got to not only wear an amazing animatronic prosthetic but I got to drive a brand new sports car for the night. The second is the opening sequence of the 5th series of the Sarah Jane adventures, where I play the Metal kind. The entrance of my character read so well in the script, where I crash land to earth with a huge explosion into a scrap metal yard and then appear from all the wreckage. The overall design of the prosthetics and costume looked so great on camera in my opinion and I loved bringing him to life. As I mentioned earlier I have so many favourite moments and characters that I've played I could end up listing them all! I do enjoy the whole process from reading the scripts, seeing the designs of the characters to filming the scenes and of course, not to mention that I have got to work alongside Christopher Eccleston, David Tenant, and Matt Smith who are also known as the Doctor. They have all brought the Doctor to life in their own individual way and it has been such a pleasure to work with them over the years. So I hope now you can understand why it is so hard for me to choose one as a favourite but I'm sure as a viewer of these programmes you will have your own favourite character as there are so many to choose from, whether that be a Cyberman, the Judoon captain or even Ood Sigma to mention but just a few.

I have never been one to give any information away about up and coming episodes of 'Doctor Who', as to me it would be like telling someone what you had brought them for charismas and I love surprises at Christmas. But what I will say is that 'Doctor Who' will be celebrating its 50th anniversary in 2013 of which will be very exciting and I'm very much looking forward to it!

All the special FX companies I've had the pleasure of working with including the amazing Millennium FX; with Neil Gorton, Rob Mayor and all the talented technicians I've encountered over the years have definitely made playing these roles a lot easier for me. The process from designing, sculpting, moulding, fabrication and the making of these wonderful characters is huge and takes a lot of people a lot of time before we get to see the finished product on our TV screens. Quite often I'm at the mercy of all the technicians as it is their wealth of knowledge and understanding of costume building, that makes the suits so comfortable and easy to wear.

This year I had the pleasure of working on the opening ceremony of the Olympic games, this is probably the biggest thing I've ever been a part of with a cast of thousands. Is there anything bigger than the Olympics? I don't think there is! I auditioned for Toby Sedgwick who is a movement director and became one of his movement assistants for his segments in the opening ceremony, of which was a large task for anyone to take on. Toby is very well known for his wealth of knowledge in actor's movement and would explain to us the type of movement the professionals and volunteers would be doing as non-verbal communication.

My time working on the Olympics with Toby and the rest of his team was amazing, an experience and part of my life that I will never forget. Everybody had such an awful amount of knowledge and experience to share of which they did and I ended up learning much more than I thought I would on the job. To see and hear the world's reaction to the show was astounding and made me very proud of what was achieved by everybody. We basically had a period of time where we devised all the audition/workshop material and discuss the different types of people we were looking for. We then did the auditions seeing hundreds of people at a time, teaching different things to different groups of volunteers and professionals that were being cast, for all the different roles within the huge show that was about to take place. After all the auditions were complete we then cracked on with devising all the sections that Toby was artistically in charge of. Because there were so many sections with so many people doing so many different types of movement, the task was at best a large one! The main rehearsal period started on the 1st of May and it was truly great. I was working with some of the hardest working, dedicated and generous people, the majority of whom had given their time for free. Being in the show and stadium on the opening ceremony will stay with me for the rest of my life.

At the beginning of 2012, I was able to fly out to Cape Town to film the new Foxy Bingo advert as Foxy is another character I play. Once I got back from Cape Town it was time to pack my bags again but this time to go to Melbourne in Australia to do a live show called The Symphonic Spectacular. Which was a live show that was very similar to the one we had done at the Royal Albert Hall in London celebrating all the 'Doctor Who' music, and where I played the Judoon Captain.

On occasions I've been asked if I would like to play roles where my face is not covered? I've always replied that I feel happy and contented playing the roles that I do but if the opportunity came about I would defiantly consider it.

Away from work I would say that I'm a very homely kind of person. I love to spend time with my family and friends. I like to be organised and kept busy of which my cats make sure of that. I'm very lucky to be able to say that I love my work and always get excited when my phone rings.

I've been playing different character roles for quite some time now whether that be a creature, monster or alien and quite often I forget what I look like until I see the reaction of the other people around me, and them backing away because their scared of what I look like!

Looking back to when I left collage in 1994, I thought to myself if I could just get a couple of jobs it would make the four years I trained for all worthwhile. I feel very privileged to have been offered the work I have and more often than not have to pinch myself to make sure it has all not been a dream.

If I was to give any advice, I would have to say what was said to me many many years ago. The world is your oyster and you must follow your hopes and dreams because with a little bit of hard work, determination and dedication you can achieve anything!

Thank you for taking the time to read my biography, I hope that it might have inspired you in some way or another.

Paul Kasey

Paul is represented by the Second Skin Agency

Paul Kasey

2 PUI FAN LEE
PO - TELETUBBIES, SHOW ME SHOW ME, FUN WITH PHONICS, CBEEBIES

The Teletubbies were never far away from the the headlines for one reason or another but it was a goliath of a show and became known worldwide and there won't be many people who can't name the four main protagonists. But as well as her time getting under the skin of Po, Pui has been a well known face on Cbeebies alongside long time compadre Chris Jarvis. It's not time for teletubbies, it's time for Pui Fan Lee!

I was lucky enough to be part of Central's Junior Television Workshop when they first set up the group, and that's where I was introduced to drama, working in telly and all other aspects of the industry, but up until then, I was just another kid bumbling around the Midlands.

For my audition for Po I remember being in a dirty old church on Tottenham Court Road and covered in dust after being asked to crawl around the floor. Very Glamourous.

I was reluctant to take the Teletubbies job at first, but as an actor, I think the general advice from everyone was, take the job, it'll be be over quickly and nobody would ever remember it!

The best thing about playing Po is that I was able to sneak a bit of Cantonese into Po's tiny vocabulary. The worst part was having to wear a massive, hot, heavy, cumbersome costume whilst running up and down the rolling hills of Tellytubby land.

It didn't take much persuasion to get back into Po's suit for the US tour though. It was New York so it wasn't difficult to decide. I remember walking down a street in Harlem (dressed as Po) and a man shouting "Only in New York!" That pretty well sums it up over there.

I enjoy presenting for children because it's honest, simple and timeless and pretty much free from cynicism.

As for my own children, my older son loves the US kids' comedies and also the off the wall cartoons like, 'The Amazing World of Gumball' which is very clever. My youngest hasn't been sucked into the tube yet but does respond to the Teletubbies strangely.. My first son came to work with me once (as Po) so that wasn't difficult to explain what mum does!

Being a mother, it's a frequent occurrence to not have a good nights sleep so when it comes to switching into TV presenter mode I can only say that we all do what we do and hope we are doing it well, whatever the world throws at us!

I've had a long friendship with Chris. He is clever, funny and kind and talented and multi skilled and I think we both have a similar outlook in life. We are often like chalk and cheese but we understand each other and laugh a lot together.

The favourite moments in my career have been starting from scratch with an idea and seeing it develop into a stage show and/or tv show is very special. Chris & I are lucky to have experienced this with the 'Chris & Pui Roadshow' and 'Show Me Show Me'. Watch out for 'Old Jack's Boat' - we first came up with the idea in a cafe in Teddington.

Pui Fan Lee,

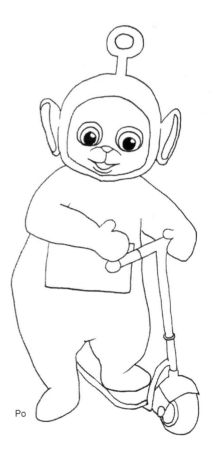

Po

"There's somebody at the door. There's somebody at the door..." went the chant in the Pink Windmill and more often than not it was Rod & Emu's larger than life, green nemesis Grotbags. To avoid incurring her wrath and being whacked with her bezazer I made sure I asked some questions that were NOT 'very personal'!

I had a wonderful childhood & a wonderful Mum. My mother Gladys (babe) Rossiter was my strong supporter! We played piano together and loved music of all descriptions. My Stepfather joined us when I was 7. Bob found me hard to handle but I loved and respected him. He was a very busy farmer but looked after me well. Thank You Bob Knight! I was a good girl sometimes but often a BRAT, but I always had a strong personality.

My mother told me that from the age of 2 I told her I would be famous on stage singing and making people laugh, nothing else entered my mind. I used to play piano and piano accordion and adored Rock 'n' Roll - and still do!

Singing from the age of 5, I had my own band at 14 years of age and mum drove us to venues until I passed my test. I studied music and was singing opera at 18.

I went on to tour Spain, Sweden, Finland and Norway and constantly toured England. I also often worked for Sir Fred Pontin at Pontins holiday centres and the largest audience was over 5,000 people. I also worked for Butlins and appeared at some outside festivals includin Fairford and The Royal show for Central TV.

My Cabaret act was singing and a few jokes mixed with having fun with my audience. Most times I didn't know what was going to happen but it was always great fun. I was a very lucky lady, fat, *hopefully* funny, and adored what I did. It was a wonderful life!

I was on the cabaret circuit for Ladbrokes at Caister Great Yarmouth when the manager of Caister, a Mr Rex Evans, gave me the name Miss Grot and it stuck!!

Rod Hull asked me to do his Emu show whilst he was at one of my holiday venues and I explained to Rod I had always wanted to be a fat fairy who got it all wrong but he asked me if I would mind being a witch instead. I agreed so long as she was not very nasty but funny.

Rod was a loyal friend and a very talented writer. Rod would always exit to the field and into his caravan to write more scripts and he wrote several books. I miss his sense of fun and his easy wit with his lovely wife Cheryl and the children. Happy memorable days.

I love Grotbags' mad dress and her great sense of fun. Grotbags was colourful and really great fun and I never any bad feelings from anyone. I had 16 years of happy life with Rod and Emu and a great TV camera crew and will always have cherished, happy memories. Thank you to all the children who wrote to me with such affection and respect.

I last performed as Grotbags on TV in 2004. The last Grotbags series was my own series with some fantastic puppets. As I own

Carol as Grotbags

Grotbags, I still have the complete costume and the BEZAZER! All her accessories are in a special box with her wigs.

If I could use my Bezazer today I'd use it to stop all the trouble in the world and stop the rain for a while. Also to stop the drug taking that is ruining so many young lives. So sad.

These days I find "BRATS" are still sometimes rude and disrespectful. As for Emu, Toby (Rod Hull's son) is doing a magnificent job, his dad would be so proud and I still love Emu very dearly.

During 42 years in showbusiness I've worked with Morecambe and Wise, Tommy Cooper, Max Wall, Arthur Askey, Bob Monkhouse, Sacha Distell, Ella Fitzgerald, Les Dawson, Brooke Benton, Brotherhood of Man, Des O'Connor, The Four Tops, Brenda Lee, Lenny Henry and Jim Davidson and my personal highlights have been meeting the Royal Family at a Children's Variety Show, Princess Margaret twice and Princess Anne 3 times. I made her a cup of tea in the VIP tent. A lovely lady. I called her a banana while I was doing Cabaret in Blazers of Windsor! She was wearing a bright yellow dress with huge puffed up sleeves and she was most gracious. At The Royal Agriculture Show I met H.M. Queen Elizabeth and HRH The Duke of Edinburgh. Long live all our Royals!

Carol Lee Scott

2 CHRISTOPHER LILLICRAP

PLAYBOARD, WE'LL TELL YOU A STORY, FLICKS, RAINBOW, EL NOMBRE

One of the great storytellers of the 70s and 80s. I first remember Christopher alongside Mo & Hedge on Playboard. He went on to have a number of his own programmes and has always been heavily involved in writing for stage and screen including an award winning musical. Whatever programme you remember Christopher from, you'll never forget his name.

There were a couple of teachers who were a big influence in my childhood. The very first thing I ever did in Primary School was when a particular teacher decided they would record a radio programme and asked me to do a little bit for it. I think it was called the 'Lillicrap Special' and it was a big hit and that started me off. When I went to grammar school I played the The Major General in a production of 'The Pirates of Penzance' and it was a big success and in the sixth form you think you're going to be a star. I was going off to be an English teacher, but two of the teachers took me to one side at the after show party and got me in a corner and said 'if you stay just being a teacher we will personally find you and kill you! You MUST go into the theatrical profession.' For a teacher at a grammar school to say that was a big thing because they usually say to get a proper job and all that, so they had a big influence. There was also an English teacher there called Mr. Jefferson who picked up that I had started writing things and put them in the school magazine, so it was teachers who had the biggest influence on me.

As a little kid I would go round to my Auntie's because we didn't have a television and I would watch 'Muffin the Mule', 'The Flowerpot Men' and 'Rag, Tag and Bobtail'. Those really fascinated me. I was an only child, so not having any brothers and sisters I would amuse myself by playing by myself and making up stories and that began my interest for children's stories. Then another really big influence in terms of storytelling was Johnny Morris. Not a lot of people will remember that he was 'The Hot Chestnut Man'. When I did my series called Busker I based it on what he used to do and his early story telling stuff, before he did Animal Magic, so he was a really big influence on me too.

When I got into acting it was while I was working in Rep. theatre at Nottingham Playhouse that I went for an audition for Play School, which I didn't get. I found out later that I didn't get it because they felt I was too interesting! One of the Play School directors, Judy Whitfield, was also producer for a new series called Playboard and she had seen my audition. I didn't get the job but about a week or two later I got a call asking if I could go and see Michael Cole and Cynthia Felgate about this series, so I actually ended up getting my own series 'Playboard' as a result of not getting 'Play School'.

For 'Playboard' they wanted someone who could do more than just stand there saying the words and in those days, what's interesting is the people who were employed were more than just presenters – the likes of Derek Griffiths and Brian Cant who could all do that bit more than just saying the words. They were either storytellers or writers or musicians or a combination of all those things which sort of changed after that era and it became people who could read autocue and introduce pop stars, but before that, we tended to be more performers. Playboard was my first experience of television and I was the only presenter alongside the puppets, Mo and Hedge. They were superb, we would put it together and improvised stuff around it and had a hell of a lot of fun doing it too. It was a brilliant launch for me. It was actually in the long hot summer of '76 at Lime Grove Studios. The heatwave started when we went in and finished when we came out, so I missed the hottest summer in British history because I was in the studio!

At that time my Equity name was Chris Lillicrap and I got asked to go and meet with Cynthia Felgate. Judy Whitfield said 'by the end of this meal they're going to ask you to change your name' and I was wondering what it was going to be, do they want me to be Higgins or Smith? We got to the crucial moment and she said 'there's only one thing and that's your name' but I got very defensive and didn't want to change it but she said 'Hear me out before you say it. At the moment it's Chris Lillicrap, we'd like you to change it to Christopher'

'Christopher what?'

'Christopher Lillicrap - it has three syllables and to be brutally honest, it takes the emphasis off the 'crap' so instead of Chris Lilli-CRAP it would be Chris-to-PHER Lillicrap'

'Oh, right! Fine, not a problem.'

There are quite a few things I went for and at one point some Americans asked me why on earth I didn't change my name and I said to him 'will you ever forget it?' and he said 'Ahhhhh. No!' so I said 'Exactly, there you are. You may or may not give me the part but you aren't going to forget the bloke who turned up with that name!' I do wonder what would have happened if I had changed it, maybe there were jobs I didn't get because of my name, I don't know, but, thinking about it, to succeed in children's television with that name was actually no mean feat!

I've actually ended up getting my own series on two occasions after auditions for other programmes I didn't get. The second time was when I went to audition

Christopher Lillicrap

for Rainbow. At the time they were looking for a Rod, Jane or a Freddy. I wasn't a brilliant musician, in fact they were better musicians than me, but I played my audition piece and Charles Warren picked up on that and actually gave me my own series for Thames 'We'll Tell you a Story' which I wrote 80-90% of the stories and the songs for.

'Flicks' followed on from that because they had a whole load of children's films from a particular company in America so we centred the programmes around those and we would create songs and stories around them. What parents used to like about it was that it fired the kids imagination whereas now TV has gone the other way and kids have to see everything. They don't take part. It's very strange that the rest of the world has become interactive and television has actually gone the other way. I went on to write the musical 'Monty Moonbeam's Magnificent Mission' and 'Christmas Cat and the Pudding Pirates' which I wrote with my wife and was the most successful one, but Monty Moonbeam's won a Theatrical Management Association (TMA) Award in 1991.

I'd started doing children's shows and that moved into bigger pantomimes over the last 20-odd years and I ended up playing Panto Dames for 10 years as well. That was how it progressed but I was also writing a lot of educational stuff. I'm still writing and currently I'm working with a colleague on part of an animation series for an Italian company. I've also just finished my first novel, which is a grown up novel. In tandem with that I've also been doing a lot of media training working with the likes of Surrey Police and also the North Wales Police & Fire Service. It's a totally separate and different career and I've worked on some high profile things at the moment, such as coaching and mentoring as a result of the Leveson Inquiry. In the early days I had also quite a bit to do with the Milly Dowler case when that all happened.

People ask me how can I do something like that, but it's quite easy. What I've found with British television is they do put you in a box, once you're in that box. Looking back, I was probably the only one who did children's television for both the BBC and ITV over a consistent period of time. In those days you were either a BBC person or an ITV person, you just went from job to job, but the BBC didn't expect you to work for ITV and vice versa, but I was unusual, because if you look back at the people like Brian and Derek and the 'Rainbow' gang, they only ever worked for one side or the other. I also worked on a religious programme for the beeb on their Sunday morning slot but at the same time I was also working on my own series for Thames and that was unusual, I don't think anyone else did that, but itt was great to be able to do that. There was a point around 1984-5 where I remember looking in the Radio Times and I was on more times than Wogan! With the two showings a day that we got (one being just before 'Rainbow') we actually got 7.5 million viewers one week.

That, today, would be a major successful programme whereas in those days that was average. At the time BBC Breakfast had launched itself it was boasting that it had got 1 million viewers and I sat there thinking that I used to get 7 times that, but I don't get any publicity for it.

The first time I played a Pantomime dame was probably one of the highlights for me. It was Mother Goose with Keith Chegwin and the reviews I got saying I was one of the best Dames in the country but another was way back, when I did my first series for Thames TV. The Controller at the time saw I was away doing musical cabaret in Denmark with my wife and I got a phone call saying ' the children's controller has just seen your series and wants it to go every week of the year, so we're going to make a lot more programmes' because she loved it so much, and I thought 'my God, I'm going to be huge'. Then the ITV strike happened, the Controller went and someone else came in and it didn't happen like that in the end. We still did 5 series, but just not every week of the year! But those were really good times and I'm proud of a lot of them and it's amazing how many people actually remember them. What's also amazing is how for certain people of a certain generation they seem to have those types of programmes as part of their consciousness. The number of people who remember Mo & Hedge and all that is quite extraordinary. Even people on my media training courses, particularly the older ones – sadly!

My son really takes the mick out of me because he's recently got married and his new wife, who's a nurse, went into work one day and one of the matrons on the ward had asked her 'what's your name going to be when you get married?' and she said 'I'll be Mrs Lillicrap.' to which she replied 'Oh! There used to be a chap on the telly called Christopher Lillicrap' she said 'Yes, that's going to be my father in law' and this woman actually said to her 'Not THE Christopher Lillicrap?', 'Yes!' 'Oh my God, she's marrying the son of THE Christopher Lillicrap..' and, of course, they won't let me forget that now, I'm THE Christopher Lillicrap and they think that's hysterical.

Christopher Lillicrap

For more information on Chris's Media Training company please visit www.ppcmedia.tv

MARIA MORGAN

A HANDFUL OF SONGS

A Handful of Songs was Maria's first foray into TV and while she sang songs such as Supercalifragilisticexpialidocious she didn't go on to be Mary Poppins, but she appeared in Les Miserables and other West End shows and ended up playing Evita instead! Maria & Keith were a natural pairing and their popularity remains as strong as ever.

I first discovered that I wanted to be a singer at a very young age. Rosalinda, my sister, was always a talented singer in her own right, and I can remember from about the age of three listening and joining in with her when she sang. As such, when I went to school, I - and, fortunately for me, the teachers as well - was always ready to give rein to my voice. Fearlessly, at the age of about five, if it rained and the children were kept indoors, the teacher used to stand me on a desk and I would sing to the kids to keep them quiet!

When I was at secondary school, I burst into the school choir and at fifteen sang with The Geoff Gough dance band at well known local venues such as Chesford Grange. By then, my sister had won 'Opportunity Knocks' three times. Her career took off and she went to live in London while the rest of the family remained in Royal Leamington Spa. It was a small town that didn't really have much to offer a star-struck child and I longed to follow in my sister's footsteps. My mother eventually sold up when I was seventeen and we moved to Staines-on-Thames to be near my sister and, in the longer term, to give me the opportunity to pursue my career.

To earn money, I started working as a secretary for a law firm doing conveyance and litigation for a while, however my sister knew that I wanted to get started in showbusiness. One day she saw an advert from The Playboy Club in 'The Stage' newspaper, looking for women who wanted to be Bunny Girls. My mother did not approve, associating the Bunny Girls with the nude magazines, but the job didn't entail any of the less salubrious activities associated with Playboy. The girls were respected and the inspectors and floor managers would make sure of this. The advert attracted my sister's attention because it mentioned that successful candidates who were actresses, singers, dancers and models would be given up to six weeks off for showbusiness work and furthermore the pay was good. Finally, having convinced my mother that there was nothing to worry about, Rosalinda went with me to see to the open auditions. Candidates were shown a film of the whole set up of Playboy and had to do an IQ test to see whether they would be better suited as a croupier or a cocktail bunny. I could not believe it when I got the job! I became a croupier Bunny Girl and it was one of the happiest times of my life. One of the highlights of my time there was the staff parties that were held in the Playboy disco, which took place about three times a year. The man responsible for PR, John Wooloughan,(who is still a good friend to this day), would arrange cabaret shows for the staff by the staff. Everyone was nominating each other and one girl said 'Oh, Maria can sing' as she had often heard me singing to myself in the dressing room while we were getting ready. So I sang at one of these parties in the first year I was there and it brought the place down. All the staff were on their feet - it was really amazing.

Word started to spread about what I was capable of, people were talking about me and interest in my career began to spark. In a short space of time, I attended my first major audition and it was for Mike Hurst who was reforming 'The Springfields'. I was chosen out of hundreds of girls. I was going to be the modern Dusty and instead of being called 'The Springfields' the band would be known just as 'Springfield'. We started recording and the line up of the group would be Mike Hurst, Keith Field and myself. At that time Keith was also appearing on the children's television programme 'A Handful of Songs'. Keith's co-presenter had just left and the producer Muriel Young was looking for a new girl to front the show with him. Keith mentioned me to Muriel as a possibility. Apparently she had seen about 70 people already including big names such as Lyndsey De Paul and Tina Charles, but she hadn't found anyone who had the connection with children that she was looking for. What she saw in me was a bubbly young girl with a little bit of glamour, without overt sex appeal but also not an Auntie type who would speak down to the children. I did a screen test and she thought I was the one! At that time, I had never even studied as an actress before, let alone been in a studio and in front of cameras. Undaunted, I recorded a mock programme with Keith, playing to camera as though it was a person, and never looked back. What was initially going to be one series turned out to be 8 years (we recorded 7 years and the last was repeats). I was about 20 when I started on the show and recorded about 379 episodes in total. There were only 3 TV channels in those days and we had between 3 to 11 million viewers depending on holidays, which was a lot for children's programmes in those days.

The shows were recorded live and they were never stopped unless there was a technical error, or perhaps a guitar string broke. We would have a stagger-through rehearsal, a full rehearsal and then the real thing. In the stagger-through, Keith and I would go through our script and music, choosing song keys and suchlike and the camera crew would plan the shots with the director. Then we'd just go for it - that's how it progressed to save time. In those days most children's programmes were budget programmes and time was of the essence. We usually recorded two shows every fortnight and sometimes three. Occasionally, recording fell on a day when a programme needed to be transmitted, so we would record one and the other would go out live. Some of the live shows could be a bit touch and go. Normally this was more the case for the technical team than for me and Keith but we did suffer a few bloopers!

Recording had to stop once when I was showing a picture of a grandfather clock which a boy had submitted as a request for Hickory Dickory Dock. I can't remember the boy's full name but let's call him Timothy Smith. I said "Look at Timothy's big brown cock [gasp] CLOCK!" and carried on as if nothing had happened, though inside I was thinking 'What are we going to do?' It wasn't me who went to pieces, though. Keith managed to hold it together with me, but the whole camera crew went to pieces. A girl sitting on a stool talking about a cock was just too much for them to bear - they couldn't keep the camera steady and started taking more shots of the ceiling than of me and Keith!

There was another unfortunate occasion in the very first series when we used to have cue cards. I said the words, "And this week I've had piles and piles...... of pictures!" (written on the next card!) Keith found it very funny and that actually stayed in the finished programme, much to my horror! But that's live TV for you.

"...new songs and blue songs and songs to bring you, happiness, no more no less..."

One other stand-out mishap came when I had an idea to use a jack-in-the-box in an episode. Muriel Young was all for new ideas involving props. I was turning its handle and it was playing 'Half a pound of tuppeny rice', when at the end of the song, up popped the Jack – which punched me in the chin! I was crying with laughter and I thought they would record the programme again, but Muriel said "No! No! It's lovely, it shows you're real and it's very funny" Keith didn't think it should be kept in and was quite annoyed. He was probably right but I laughed so much it hurt.

We would get sacks of mail every week and I would get lots of post from grown up males as well as children, which the secretary found very amusing. Some were a bit perverted. I remember one guy asking if I could wear a red ribbon around my neck on the programme for him - "I'm a night worker and I can't help having the programme on every Friday lunch time, you're in my dreams." A lot of adults knew who I was besides the stay-at-home housewives, either because their work meant they were at home during the day or from seeing the programme during their holidays. So I became 'the girl from A Handful of Songs' rather than Maria Morgan because the show became so well known. I was very proud to be part of it. We would get thousands of paintings from children and would never single any one effort out for being better than another. We believed, and I still do to this day, that a young child, when doing a drawing for you, no matter how talented or untalented they might be, do their best. We chose pictures at random for the requests. They were interesting to say the least. Some were lovely, some were funny and some we had to use our imagination to work out what they were! Keith and I really could relay our enthusiasm and encouragement, because it was genuine and we knew how much praise meant to our little viewers. Among the sacks full of pictures, we even had mail from royalty. Of course, we couldn't disclose where they came from and just referred to 'the little princes/princesses'.

Keith is a great bloke, very clever with a great sense of humour and took over the writing of the programmes after a few series. He was also very quick changing tunes and keys and always fair in alternating songs. We knew hundreds of children's songs. We sang some pop songs too, but they had to be innocent, like 'Save Your Kisses For Me' by Brotherhood of Man and 'Yellow Submarine' by The Beatles. It was a varied programme. One song that we used to perform was 'Rupert the Bear' and I eventually recorded a pop version, which met with some success. It appealed to all ages and in fact there was a DJ on Radio 1 who used to use the beginning of it to open his programme.

Whilst appearing on 'A Handful of Songs' I continued to work for Playboy, travelling to Granada TV in Manchester to record the TV programmes every fortnight. In my third year there I was asked to work at The Clermont Club in Berkeley Square, which was owned by Playboy, but was a separate entity. As croupiers we dressed in elegant Jean Muir dresses and I mixed with all kinds of people. I met Lord Lucan, James Goldsmith, Cubby Broccoli to mention but a few. Everyone who was anyone, either notorious or with lots of money, came there. I saw another side to life where money didn't mean anything. I dealt black jack, punto banco, and roulette, where millions would pass through my hands. It was an eye-opening experience.

It was while working there that I met the owner of President Records, Edward Kassner, who would occasionally come to The Clermont. He was very interested in my career as a singer having seen me perform on the television. and offered me a recording contract. President Records were riding high with artists like K.C and The Sunshine Band and George McCrae so I thought it would be a good label to sign to. My career as a recording artist never quite reached the heights I would have hoped for but it brought me good fortune in a different aspect as ultimately, I married David, the son of Edward Kassner, who was producing my first record. We went on to have two children, a son and a daughter who I love very much. My son Alexander became a banking lawyer after university but opted for a career change and is now working with David in the family music publishing business – Kassner Associated Publishers Limited. Natalie, my daughter, was always very interested in fashion and now works promoting Harrods in their Media Sales and Marketing team for the beauty division. Alex remembers me being on television. He was born while I was in A Handful of Songs, so when he was very young he that thought that every mummy was on television. Natalie came along after I played Evita in the West End.

I remember the fun times I had when working in pantomime; the bond within the cast members and the interaction with the audiences. Little and Large headlined my first panto and they were hilarious. The pantomime was 'Aladdin' in which I played the Princess and Aladdin was played by Patsy Ann Scott who together with Talli Halliday playing the genie, became the 'three amigos'. I shared digs with the dancers, one being my understudy. This funny girl was Tracy Ullman who became one of our most celebrated comediennes. Another outstanding memory was when I played Cinderella. The real coach of Queen Victoria was hired to drive me, dressed in the ball gown, around the streets of Maidstone to promote the pantomime.

It was very hard being a mum, housewife and an artiste at the same time during a non-stop career of about 20 years. I took a short break from showbusiness in the late-90s but then never got back to the same level I had left at. I've now formed my own company designing wedding dresses and providing one-to-one bridal services. I just love it. The beautiful gowns remind me of the dreams I had when I was young of being a Disney Princess and also take some inspiration from the costumes I wore on stage, especially the amazing white dress I wore for the balcony scene in Evita singing 'Don't Cry For Me Argentina'.

Whilst the wedding business is picking up nicely, if any opportunity in show business were to present itself now, I'd still jump at it. Singing and dancing is in my blood and will always have a pull. I'd also love to do some straight acting, as I feel I never fully explored that part of my talents, except for TV commercials. I had some very good critiques from The Central School of Speech and Drama where I trained and from Dorothy Black with whom I first trained, but when I started auditioning, my voice was always the main point of interest and so I ended up in musicals.

'Snoopy' was my first musical, playing the part of Peppermint Patty. She was fantastic - I loved her tomboy character. The show just had a cast of seven but it was such a happy cast. Zoe Bright, Melanie Parr and I made up a little trio of cartoon trouble. One night I got carried away in my tomboy character and pushed Melanie off into the wings of the stage in a playful song. Zoe and Melanie laughed uncontrollably off stage, leaving me to finish the song on my own! The audience howled with laughter and thought it all part of the show. I have so much affection for 'Snoopy' and I still sing a couple of songs from it today. It was a lovely production.

After 'Snoopy' ended, I began auditioning for the lead in 'Evita'. Following one set of auditions (two years before I eventually joined the cast) I was told I had the part but within a week lost it because the actress playing Eva Peron decided to retract her decision to leave. Wanting to progress my career, I joined the band Wall Street Crash. The band was doing very well at the time, being seen on TV all over Europe. It had its own series in Italy and TV specials in Holland, plus guest appearances on shows in the UK such as 'The Val Doonican Show' and 'The Mike Read Show'. I really enjoyed being part of a band. There were two girls and four boys and we were the first ever real singing & dancing group. After a year, though, the West End called me back, and this time when I was told I had the part of Evita it was for real.

As was customary for 'Evita', two girls would share the title role, in this case me and Kathryn Evans. She played the majority of performances and I played 2 to 3 a week unless she had time off in which case I would perform them all. I was coming up to the end of my first year when David Land and Bob Swash, the producers, said that I'd be taking over Kathryn's role as 'Evita 1' as she was preparing to leave and another girl would take my place as 'Evita 2'. Unfortunately, as I prepared for what would have been a fantastic step in my career, the cast got the devastating news that Evita would be closing within two weeks as Tim Rice wanted to bring in 'Chess' to The Prince Edward theatre where Evita was playing. I will always feel that this was a terrible piece of luck and definitely dampened my career progression, though a few years later I bounced back and played the part of Fantine in 'Les Miserables'..'I Dreamed A Dream' is still my favourite of the songs that I have performed.

Nevertheless, if I am known for anything it will still always be 'A Handful of Songs'. Even to this day I have the odd person stop me in the street and ask if I have presented a children's programme. Sometimes I ask how they recognise me. Most people say firstly it's my smile and secondly my voice hasn't changed! I will always look back on my career with pride and pleasure. I shall always be indebted to my family and friends who helped me along the way, especially my Mother who gave me so much love and support. That is why I persisted and kept going. That, and the fact I'm infected with that bug they call show-biz. It has always been there and still is. Watch this space!

Maria Morgan

To find out more about Maria's bridal service please visit
www.yourweddingdressuk.com

ERKAN MUSTAFA
ROLAND BROWNING - GRANGE HILL

There can't be many children who didn't watch Grange Hill at some point in their childhoods as it graced our screens for 30 years and Erkan played one of its most famous and recognisable pupils. Being a chubby, bespectacled school kid myself I felt quite an affinity with the trials and tribulations of Roland Browning but what was it like auditioning for that school?

Well, I remember my audition very well even though it was so long ago. I went into it never having any formal training, this was the first one that I'd ever been to. Going into the room, I was scared but the first person I had set eyes was one of my brothers mates, we didn't know that we were both going to audition, but I felt at ease straight away. They handed us a script and asked us to read the parts that we were going for. We both had to read it twice and that was it really. Some weeks later my mum had a letter asking for me to go back for another. There must have been more than 30 children going up for many parts we were put into groups to act out scenes and we spent the whole morning doing stuff like that. We were asked to come back one by one to read, then we were told if we had the part. Yes! I'd got it! I remember coming home on the train shocked as this was 'Grange Hill' - the biggest children show on television.

Being in a show like 'Grange Hill' had an effect on my schooling as you have so much time doing the shows, all the children had to do work on set but it was hard to concentrate for me as I felt lost at first, but then you just get in the swing of it all. My school was very good to me, making sure that I got all the work that my peers were doing but yet it was hard. As a child actor who still went to normal school, it was difficult. First you had your class mates asking questions all the time and also some of the kids were very jealous of what I was doing. I was lucky, being the person that I am, I could handle things like this. I had fights about it, but looking back now I guess it was all part of growing up and finding your identity in your teenage years. Over all, my own schooling was very different from Rolands as I had many friends and took part in everything I could; sports, trips, drama club and music clubs. I played both rugby and football for my school, some thing that Roland would never do. It was only later in the show that we see Roland playing basketball which I found funny as he was the best at it.

During my time on the show we had some great times away from it, we did loads of stuff for charities which I still try to do today. Giving your time gives me so much joy. As most people know, we had the chance to go to the USA to meet the then President's wife Nancy Reagan to tell her what the kids of Grange Hill were doing in the UK regarding the 'Just Say No' campaign, which she was the patron of. What an amazing experience it was for me as well the rest of the cast who had the opportunity to go, one I will never forget.

Looking back now I feel it was a privilege to be in a show that had such an effect on peoples lives. Before 'Grange Hill' kids didn't have a show to relate to. If I can remember back, children's shows were all cartoons, magazine style shows and drama, there was never a show that kids could talk about the next day in their own schools. As 'Grange Hill' covered so many topics that were happening in schools up and down the country; racism, bullying, teenage pregnancy, disabilities and of course drugs, I feel it captured so many people's hearts - we all went to school and could relate to some kind of story line that 'Grange Hill' was showing.

Looking back on my time on the show it has left me with so many memories some of which will stay with me forever. I had my first kiss with someone on the show and we still speak form time to time. The people that I worked with back then all had some part of my teenage years so, yes I had some great times and met so many people that are still part of my life in some way or the other. My personal highlight of playing Roland was the fact that he had an effect on so many people, over the years. I have had numerous amounts of people come and say how much Roland was like them, how had they had been bullied just like him and it showed that they were not alone. If playing Roland helped just one person then I must have been doing some thing right. Today Roland is living in France running a bakery with his French wife, he would be helping children to cope with bullies and helping them with confidence issues, weight problems and teaching basketball in his spare time. He would also be writing to Gripper Stepson in prison and helping with his anger management problems!

After 'Grange Hill' I tried to carry on being an actor, but the transference from child actor to adult actor was difficult for me. I would go to audition and people were just asking about my time on the show and not really looking at what I could do. I did do some bits of work but it was not for me really. I bummed around for many years in different jobs, but the passion to get back into it has been too much. I have always loved writing, be it comedy drama etc, so this year I have had some work commissioned and I look forward to seeing that on our screens. Who knows, I might even get back into doing some acting. we will have to wait and see.

Erkan Mustafa

HUGO MYATT

TREGUARD - KNIGHTMARE

Welcome, watchers of illusion, to the castle of confusion! Knightmare was a hugely popular fantasy adventure game show for children. This virtual reality show used new technology and was ground breaking at the time. The show was presented by the iconic dungeon master Treguard (of Dunshelm) but what of the man beneath that magnificent facial hair? Enter stranger.

The part of Treguard came rather out of 'left field'. 'Knightmare' was made at Anglia Television. I knew Tim Child, the creator of 'Knightmare', only slightly. He was a journalist and programme director in Anglia's news division. I had done a few bits and bobs for Anglia. Tim approached me and asked whether I would be interested in doing a pilot for a new show idea. He explained it was only experimental and that the pilot would not be broadcast. It was just to see if the idea was feasible. Well it sounded like fun so we met up and he explained the whole concept. I did not understand a word of it but being an actor I said that of course I could do it. We made the pilot and I began to understand a little bit more. We actually made a second and longer experimental pilot. After that I dismissed it from mind as I assumed that if the idea were taken up it would not involve me. One day I had a call from Tim. He said, "We have a series." I said "Well done." "No," he said. "WE have a series. They want you."

At the time I wasn't so much flattered to be thought of as making a good dungeon master, as just terrified. The whole thing was so novel that none of us really knew how it would pan out. As for the Dungeon Master I had no idea whether the character I created would work at all.

Treguard's costume and look of the series were down to the designers. Treguard's character developed over the eight series. Initially I had to supply the conflict. Treguard's character had to be slightly menacing and mysterious as well as offering guidance. This was quite a delicate balance as I didn't want to be so frightening as to intimidate the children neither did I want them to think that I might trick them. They had to know that whatever I said could be trusted. Later the character of Pickle, played by David Learner, was introduced. Pickle, as my faithful elf, allowed us to comment on the action, and so subtly give the kids more clues. When Jackie Sawiris as Majida was introduced she was a feisty character and quite prepared to 'talk back' to Treguard and so making him less intimidating. Finally with the introduction of our archenemy, Lord Fear, inimitably played by Mark Knight, we had our villain and so Treguard was able to ease back the menacing aspect of his character.

Over eight years there are too many memorable moments to list. It is not always appreciated that, although the programmes were recorded they were made as if live. That is to say there were no rehearsals and no retakes with the children or it wouldn't have been a real contest. What the viewer saw on the screen is what actually happened. This made it very exciting, as none of us knew what would happen next. Whatever scenarios we predicted might happen the kids always came up with something we hadn't thought of. If I were to have my own dungeon now I'd put in more brilliant kids to be Dungeoneers and Advisors. Game On!

I was and am principally a stage actor and director and at the time had been for twenty years. Over my career I have acted in nearly 200 stage shows and directed about fifty. I have appeared in 38 pantomimes and eight seasons as Chairman of Music Hall as well as a smattering of television and films. I have also had a long career as a voiceover artiste. I had *"Ooooh,* tried a couple of 'proper' jobs but my 'Walter Mitty' imagination *Nasty."* would not let me settle. Acting seemed to be the only honest *Treguard* career for me. As an actor having a beard is not conducive to getting cast unless you are Brian Blessed. I grew the beard twice a year, once for pantomime, where I inevitably played the villain, and then again for the recording of Knightmare otherwise I was clean-shaven. This meant I was rarely recognised in the street but frequently the voice gave me away at supermarket checkouts and the like.

Everything has been a highlight as far as I am concerned. For forty plus years it has all been great fun.

A last word on Knightmare. I should like to pay a tribute to all the other actors who took part. In many ways their job was harder than mine. They had to interact directly with the Dungeoneer and without a script. It was all improvisation. This is more difficult than it sounds because in improvisation it is very easy to go off at a tangent. These actors had to improvise and yet still keep the game and the particular scenario they were playing on track. They all have my greatest admiration.

Hugo Myatt

NIGEL PLASKITT

PIPKINS, NEW CAPTAIN SCARLETT, POTAMUS PARK, ROUND THE BEND,
SPOOKS OF BOTTLE BAY, MOPATOPS SHOP

For people of a certain age (like myself) Pipkins is a classic of its time. Over 300 episodes were made with Hartley the Hare and the gang. For Nigel it was the start of his puppetry and voice career that has gone onto include Spitting Image, The Muppet Christmas Carol, Round the Bend, Captain Scarlett, Peppa Pig Live and Avenue Q... and an often quoted advert!

I started playing around with voices when I was a child. I used to do shows in the living room with a washing line strung up across the room – the things my poor parents used to put up with - and I played different characters then, so I was always interested in doing that kind of thing. We didn't have a TV when I was a kid, not until I was about 10 because no one really had TVs in the 50s so we used to listen to the radio a lot. I did watch TV at neighbours and my grandparents had a TV so it was Rag, Tag and Bobtail, Andy Pandy and that sort of programme when I was young and from about 10 onwards it was things like 'Doctor Who', which I ended up being in as well, which was great. I went on to play Unstoffe in 'The Ribos Operation' alongside Tom Baker.

I'd done a little bit of puppetry when I was a kid and worked at the Little Angel Theatre in Islington in my school holidays and worked there very briefly before I went to college full time but that was it really. There wasn't any training you could do, you were just thrown in at the deep end. I'd not planned to do it professionally, I just fell into it.

I actually started out to be an actor, that's the route I wanted to travel down. I was able to do 'Pipkins' for about 6 months of the year and then I could go away and do smaller acting jobs, one of which was the famous Vicks 'Malcolm' TV commercials but I think that got wanting to be famous out of my system. It was certainly after that I'd had my taste of fame and thought maybe this isn't what I wanted.

Even now, very occasionally, even though it's 40 years ago, some people still remember the ad and some people even remember the lines from it. I'm surprised that people still recognise me from it, but they do, and if they don't, then when they know it was me who did it, they'll always know one or two lines from it, which is remarkable after such a long time.

Vicks realised it was a good advert, originally we had to cut it two ways as the director had an idea how he wanted to shoot it. This was only my second or third job and Barbara New, who played my mother, was more experienced and very supportive. About half way through the morning I could see these groups of creatives getting into huddles with the director and I thought I'd blown it, but he came back to me and said 'they're very worried that we're treating this commercial as a comedy' which is actually what he wanted, 'it's a medical commercial and we shouldn't make it too jokey but I've managed to persuade them to let me shoot it both ways' so for every shot we did, we did one with a more serious intent and for the other one we'd go over the top, saying 'bum' instead of 'mum' and things like that. He cut them both together and showed them and fortunately they went with the slightly comic ones and I think that's what caught everyone's imagination.

'Pipkins' came about because I knew the wife of the designer of the programme for many years, and when he started to design the programme she came to me and said 'you do character voices, don't you?' and I said yes. 'There's this programme my husbands designing for ATV', and she was making the puppets. So I had a strange meeting with Michael Jeans who was the producer and director of it. It wasn't really an audition because he never asked me to do any voices he said "do you think you can do a voice for Hartley the Hare?" and he showed me the character description and I said "Oh yeah I think I can do that" and that was it. I got the job. It was 1971 and there was nobody doing very much in the way of TV puppets because there was very little afternoon or daytime TV at that point, if anything at all.

The character of Hartley himself came out of thin air, I think panic probably more than anything helped create him when confronted with the script! I did have a breakdown of how Michael saw the character and what he was like, but if you look at the only episode that survives from the second series, he's a changed character 3 or 4 years later on as I'd gradually developed the character and established it more, so it's quite interesting from my point of view watching that. I hadn't seen the early ones until fairly recently and when we started doing the DVDs, not only do I see my technique develop quite dramatically in those few years but also the character changed as I got more established and confident. It's a joy, in a way, to have the ability to do a character over a number of years and develop something like that.

There was one episode when Hartley had his own puppet and sings a song to him which was good fun to do. We called Hartley's puppet Michael after Michael Jeans, that was my little joke. Also there was a kind of word play with 'don't take the michael' I think I said 'don't take my michael' but those were the sorts of gentle bits of adult humour we put in, hoping that it would be interesting for adults to watch as well so that it would encourage them to sit and watch it with their children. The writer's never intentionally put in any innuendo into the script, there were one or two things that I ad-libbed, you can usually tell that because at the end of the scene there would be a gap, expecting the scissors to be put in or some comment made, but he liked it so he kept it in and that did happen occasionally on some of the episodes that have survived. When we got more established that was more likely to happen.

Back then we had more time to make the programmes. We had three days rehearsals for two programmes, so we recorded two programmes a week and half a day out of that rehearsal I would record the voice overs for all the narrator bits and then we'd have a day in the studio to record the show, but we'd record it in sections. I know that 'Rainbow' had to edit as they went, but we had the luxury of edit time, but I don't know why, so the director could take the tapes away and edit the show afterwards.

Not many of the 330-odd episodes that we did have survived, sadly. I enjoyed the character more in the last 4 or 5 years as I was more confident. It was great to work with a load of different people, although I was the only kind of constant throughout the whole 9 years all the other characters came and went with different people playing them, most of whom I'm still in touch with, so that's great. We had three different presenters, all totally different in their styles.

Out of them all I guess one of my favourites was the glove puppet episode and there was another one called 'Cowboys' which was a great episode where Heather Tobias, who was playing pig, did some great stuff.

It was on 'Pipkins' I met Sue Nicholls when she joined the show in the late 1970s [as Mrs Muddle]. We got on really well and we've stayed in touch ever since and meet up regularly. Coincidentally she married somebody else that I knew. My second job was a tour for Bill Kenwright called "Conduct Unbecoming." It was a drama and playing one of the lead roles was Mark Eden who ended up playing Alan Bradley in Coronation Street and is now married to Sue. It was quite a coincidence.

I think the way television for small children is made has changed dramatically, usually there's no or very little rehearsal time. We went through a terrible phase through the 80s and 90s where everything had to be fast, fast, fast, cut, cut, cut all the time and shout, shout, shout at the audience or they wouldn't pay attention, but in actual fact, I've heard people say that some of that was to do with the fact that they felt that the attention span of the child had reduced, which is absolute nonsense of course as children are children still, and that's proven by the fact that if you watch an episode of Pipkins it is probably a slower pace than many programmes now, but I've had many many emails since the DVDs went out from people, having shown the DVDs to their own children, who say they just want more. They are not worried at all by the fact that it's a slower pace.

What I always feel about 'Pipkins' is that for a pre-school audience, there certainly wasn't anything before that was like this and I don't think there's been anything since that actually gives little 10 minute dramas, which is what they were, that has a story and has tensions between the characters, there isn't anything else for 3-5 year olds that's been like that. Michael Jeans was ahead of his time when he thought it up and I think people have been scared to do anything like that since. A lot of programmes now are basically colour and movement for young audiences. There's no real, what I'd call 'drama' for pre-school children any more and I think that's one of the things that we supplied and I suspect it has influenced two or three generations of children in it's 9 year run because of the people that have told me that some of the things we did in the programme, they felt, influenced what they did in later life. A friend of mine who was in the original audience remembers us making a stagecoach and after seeing the programme he went away and made a model himself and he ended up being a model maker in his professional life and he thinks that might well have stimulated his interest in creating things. That's what we tried to do, without doing a Blue Peter 'here's one I made earlier', just simple stuff you could do at home or something to encourage children to play and make things up.

When you're making the programmes you don't think about the influence you'll have on people in later life. I certainly didn't when I did 'Pipkins' because I was doing a daily job and in those days you didn't have any feedback. They did get letters and occasionally Michael would show us one of them but I don't think we saw half the stuff that came in, but now, of course, it's all on the internet and interestingly on the Pipkins website **www.pipkins.net** I've put a link on there saying 'write to me with your memories' and I regularly get people who come across the site and write back and let me know what they thought and I always write back. It's interesting to know that a) there was somebody out there and b) that they remember it! About two thirds of the way through 'Pipkin's we started to become aware that we had a fairly heavy student viewership as well, so we were getting a lot of 18-19 year olds watching it and it had already become a culty thing because it was so off the wall and there was nothing else like it on TV. 'Rainbow' and 'Mr. Trimble' were so conventional compared to what we were doing which was completely different.

As for the puppets, Michael Jeans had the original Hartley, but he died about a year ago so I would imagine he's with his family. Hopefully, one day, I might be able to persuade them to give Hartley and the tortoise to a television museum. I have a Hartley that I use for personal appearances that has been made for me in recent years. I can still get my voice up there to do Hartley's voice although it's better if I've been doing it for a while, but I deliberately made Hartley's and the tortoise's voices at different ends of the spectrum so they would sound completely different.

Nigel Plaskitt

When I did Mopatops Shop for the Henson Company about 10 years ago there were about 250 programmes with a guest in each one and I played about 200 of those guests so I had to try and find different voices for each of them. I'm not sure if I succeeded totally but I tried to get as much variety as I could.

I've done a wide variety of work and it's good to have that on the CV but it also makes me think I've been around a long time too! I've been very very lucky and done some really good stuff and all of it slightly iconic in its own way. Of all the shows I've done it means quite a lot to people and they have their own memories of it and it's very nice. There are several characters I've created that I would say are my favourites. Hartley, of course, has to be one, and maybe John Major in 'Spitting Image' and maybe the PG Tips Monkey. I've probably missed some others out but those are the three I've enjoyed the most.

It's almost impossible to say what has been the highlight of my career because when I've done jobs they've usually been big chunky jobs, 'Pipkins' was 9 years, 'Spitting Image' was 13 years, I've worked on and off for the Henson Company for a period of 15 years and I've been working as an advisor on 'Avenue Q' for 6 years, so all of them, for me, have some sort of highlight and they've all been so different. 'Spitting Image' was a great thing to do and so different from anything else you could ever conceive of using puppets. 'Avenue Q' is aimed at adults and is great to do but at the same time I'm doing the same sort of thing with the 'Peppa Pig' stage show which is another iconic thing at the moment and is a joy to work with.

What's interesting is when I've seen the TV version of 'Peppa Pig' and certainly with the stage version, I feel the pace is very similar to 'Pipkins', it isn't one of these bang, bang, bang shows with quick cuts.

I'm really proud of what we did. We had a great team of writers and a great team of performers and production team - people who I still work with today and they all remember 'Pipkins' quite fondly.

Nigel Plaskitt

To read more about Nigel's career please visit www.nigelplaskitt.com

LEE PRESSMAN
RAINBOW, T-BAG, SPATZ, FRANKENSTEIN'S CAT, GENIE IN THE HOUSE,
THE TOMORROW PEOPLE, SHAUN THE SHEEP, RASTAMOUSE...

As writers for childrens television go, Lee is up there with the most prolific, bringing characters to life for 30 years. Having started writing for Rainbow, Lee has co-created and written T-Bag and his latest work has seen him writing for Rastamouse, which some parts of the media claim has hidden drug references! So who better to ask? Is it traditional for adults to think there are drug references in children's programmes?

Absolutely traditional (and a bit boring). You can take it right back to 'Alice in Wonderland'. 'The Magic Roundabout' was always being accused of it. All I can say is, whatever anybody thinks or says, in writing 'Rastamouse' nobody ever tried to sneak in a reference to drugs. But you can't win - as soon as you say the characters like cheese (after all they are mice) somebody pops up saying cheese is just a coded reference for dope.

In my childhood I was a massive fan of Spike Milligan - his poems and stories, radio scripts, TV appearances. A wonderful, crazy, unique writer and performer. And I loved the Jennings books by Anthony Buckeridge - brilliant story telling and incredibly funny schoolboy stories set in a small private school. Many many years later I was privileged to get to know Anthony during the last years of his life and that was a great thrill. And from a very young age I was pretty obsessed with rock music - I started off listening to Radio Luxembourg every night under the bed covers on a crackly transistor radio - it was a magical experience.

One of my favourites programmes was 'The Adventures of William Tell' Not sure why but it seemed pretty exciting at the time. I loved American comedy shows and my favourite was 'Sgt Bilko' (and still is). Genius scripts and an mazing central performance from Phil Silvers. And I'm still a massive fan of all the old classic Disney movies.

When I was about nine or ten I attempted my own Jennings type novel - my version was called 'Jamie Goes To School'. Years later I discovered that when Alan Ayckbourn was a child he had also started his career by writing his own Jennings book.

When we were students we were all mad about a BBC kid's show called Playaway. A few years later I decided to submit a pile of unsolicited material - poems, songs, sketches etc. I was amazed and delighted when the producer of Playaway got back to me and said they liked some of my stuff and one joke that they particularly liked was going to be on the show the very next week. And I was paid the grand sum of £4. After that I wrote regularly for the show over the next four or five years alongside cult figures such as Johnny Ball!

T-Bag was born while I was working for Thames Television on 'Rainbow'. Marjorie Sigley the head of Thames at the time asked me to come up with an idea for a series based on letters of the alphabet. I pitched an idea called Dottie in Dictionaria about a little girl who shrinks and travels across a board game where every square was a different letter of the alphabet (I was very influenced by Lewis Carroll). T. Bag was the evil character who lived in the T Square. This developed into the long running series that we know and love, and Grant and I ended up writing all 94 episodes.

The best thing about writing for children is the freedom to let your imagination run wild. On T.Bag for instance my writing partner Grant and I spent nine years inventing the wacky world of the T.Set, sending our characters through time and space, doing spoofs of every film we'd ever seen - it was a glorious opportunity to make some of our childish fantasies come true. Now I'm writing silent scripts for sheep (Shaun the Sheep) which has to be more fun than cranking out EastEnders. I'd say the character I've written for which is most like myself is probably The Farmer in Shaun the Sheep. In looks and temperament.

With 'Rastamouse', one change that I had to be aware of was that Michael de Souza, who created the show, was a Rastafarian, and he didn't believe that any of the characters who offended should be punished. This was challenging since there was a crime being committed every week. So we had to think of ways that the wrong doer could learn a lesson and be redeemed in some positive way. As far as writing the West Indian patois most of the writers became pretty good at it.

The biggest distraction when writing used to be the phone. Now it seems to be emails. I get around thirty a day and I'm always breaking off writing to answer them. I guess if one writes at

Lee with Rastamouse

night you're less likely to be distracted. But I have to admit that if I've been at my desk all day I LOVE being distracted, and in reality phone calls are very welcome (as are excuses to leave the house, go to the shops, hoover the house - anything to avoid coming up with new story ideas).

I'm very fond of T.Bag as a character (both Tallulah and Tabatha). But I think the series 'Spatz' was the finest work that Grant and I ever produced when we were writing together. We're also very proud of our TV movie B & B. And 'The Tomorrow People' was pretty cool.

There's only the same few stories in the world, but they get told differently by every generation. I've just written a half hour Shaun the Sheep script and if you examine it it's really just a classic Western - the bad guys ride into town and take over- the hero drives them out and restores order. It's a story as old as the hills, but we're telling it with sheep.

Frankenstein's Cat

TONY ROBINSON
PLAYAWAY, SAM ON BOFF'S ISLAND, TALES FROM FAT TULIPS GARDEN,
MAID MARIAN AND HER MERRY MEN

Tony seems to have been a constant presence in my life (on television that is) From Playaway and Fat Tulips Garden in my early years, Maid Marian and her Merry Men later on and the much loved Blackadder and Time Team as I've gotten older, so I think it's fair to say I like his work!

I grew interested in working with children after I became an Arts Council Trainee Director at Midlands Arts Centre (which had its own professional childrens theatre company in the late 60s and early 70s). I took over the job from Mike Leigh! I wanted to develop a loose, relaxed, improvised feeling in my work for children, and the BBC responded positively to that.

A perfect example of this is "The Court of King Caractacus" on 'Playaway', where we deliberately tried to create the feeling that we were only getting through the song by the skin of our teeth. Can I still remember the words to it? - Nope!

The inspiration for Maid Marian occured during the time I was working in childrens television. My own children were at primary school, and my daughter Laura was a bit of a tomboy. I remember watching her playing football with the boys and thinking "If she'd been in Robin Hood's gang she would have run it."

I've always loved history since my dad used to tell me about his adventures in the Second World War. This meant I felt very at home in the various Blackadder periods, but I don't think it stoked my loved of history - it was already there.

As a child I was inspired by the Roman and Greek legends, and frankly by every book I read. The first comic I remember was an old man on telly called Mr Pastry, but my real inspiration was the Goon Show, as it was for so many of my generation.

I'm very lucky that my career has had so many highlights - being in the original cast of "Oliver!", taking over the role of the Artful Dodger, playing Anthony Newley's son in "Stop the World I want to Get Off", my first big break after drama school as Sam in "Sam on Boff's Island", running my own theatre company at the MAC, Baldrick, Maid Marian, Time Team, Worst Jobs and latterly a five year deal with Australian History Channel to make a history series for them every year for five years.

Tony Robinson

MICHAEL ROSEN

SCHOOLS TV, WALRUS, MIDDLE ENGLISH, READABOUT, YOU TELL ME,
EVERYBODY HERE, CHILDRENS LAUREATE

Micheal made frequent appearances on Schools TV and ignited children's interest in literature and poetry throughout the land. He has written several collections of humourous verse for children and topped it off by becoming the Children's Laureate in 2007, not bad for a former chicken plucker!

So, if you're trying to write some verse / And your brain is feeling frozen,
The words will begin to tumble out / When you think of Michael Rosen!

My passion for literacy and teaching came directly from my parents. They were both teachers but with their membership of professional teachers' associations and then their higher education with diplomas and doctorates, they both ended up in teacher training. My mother conducted a nationwide survey of teaching methods in primary schools with special reference to literacy and the pair of them wrote it up as a book: 'The Language of Primary School children'. Meanwhile, my father was investigating linguistics, narratology, autobiographical writing and storytelling. At home throughout my childhood, my parents were great readers, readers outloud, storytellers, joke-tellers, singers and players with language. They could both speak other languages: Yiddish, French, German and Latin. My father had studied Old English and Old Norse as well.

I was taken on by the BBC in 1969 as a General Trainee. This was a training in radio, TV and film production lasting about two and a half years with a view to getting a production job at the end of it. General Trainees were posted 'on attachment' to about four departments during that time, and one of my attachments was to Play School. 1970-71 I think.

The first performance stuff I did in front of cameras was for a BBC Schools programme with the acronym WALRUS produced by Morton Serguy. We looked at a Michael Morpurgo novel, I remember. I think he had heard about me somehow, though by then I had been sacked by the BBC on grounds of being a security risk - according to MI5. In case that all seems James Bond-like, it was all verified and admitted in 1985.

My next TV work was with Thames TV, ITV Schools television. I made a programme with Roger McGough called 'You Tell Me' based on a poetry book we wrote together. And then came 'Everybody Here' a series in the first days of Channel 4. That came about because the producer, Susanna Capon approached me to come up with an idea for a children's TV programme. I knew Susanna from the time I worked in BBC Radio Drama.

Michael reading 'We're Going on a Bear Hunt' © Seven Stories

I had worked as a chicken plucker and never thought I would one day end up as the children's laureate. Especially as I was no good at chicken plucking. Mind you, I didn't think chicken plucking was going to be my career. It was supposed to be a holiday job. But I wasn't even good enough for that!

I doubt if the levels of literacy in the 70s and 80s are much different from today. Literacy levels have never varied very much once full time compulsory education past the age of 11 came in.

It's rather hard to say where I draw my inspiration from, but it's a mixture of things I remember, hear, see or read. My poetry/literary heroes are Geoffrey Chaucer, William Shakespeare, Charles Dickens, Voltaire, Guy de Maupassant, Gerard Manley Hopkins, Erich Fried, Edward Lear, Lewis Carroll, Paul Durcan, Jackie Kay, Lemn Sissay, Li Po, Tu Fu, Langston Hughes and 'Anon' ie folk and traditional rhymes, tales and songs from all over the world. I can only remember one line from the first poem I wrote: 'And now the train is slowing down.'

My biggest achievement was the Children's Laureateship: that was an acknowledgement that I had done OK and that I had something to contribute to the effort to keep children's literature in the public eye. My proudest achievement was setting up the Roald Dahl Funny Prize, a yearly award for the funniest books of the year.

Michael Rosen

To read more about Michael's work please visit www.michaelrosen.co.uk

SID SLOANE

CBEEBIES, LET'S PLAY

When Cbeebies launched in 2002 Sid was there from the very start, but what a change of scene after he left a career in stockbroking to pursue a life as an actor. 10 years later he has a new show 'Let's Play' and with his 'Sid's Show' tour underway, I'm sure he'll be around to entertain children for many years to come.

Who or what was an influence in your childhood?

I loved running, playing outside, and family days out visiting other families. We attended church on Sunday's and mum was a community woman. Mostly, I loved playing football, we would play anytime, any place, indoors or outdoors. Having three brothers and one sister all close in age meant we could find things to do together. I loved acting out scenes from 'Puss in Boots' and 'The Three Little Pigs' which I listened to on vinyl.

You had a career in stockbroking, what made you decide to give all that up and study to be an actor?

My dad had all the Burt Lancaster, Kirk Douglas, Clint Eastwood and Charles Bronson films which I'd love watching. After a while I'd look at De Niro and Pacino and think...I get it...I can do that!

Can you tell me how you chose your stage name?

I was playing around with ideas really. Sidney Poitier inspired part of the name; his acting prowess is elegant and sublime... I want to be like him. I had some life affirming experiences in and around Sloane Street in London, so I put the two together for luck. I didn't think equity would accept my application, so when the membership arrived in the post I was wracking my brains trying to work out who, by that name, might be using my home address. Turned out to be me!

What would you say is the best part about presenting & performing for children?

There is a finite line between cheesy and super cool. With children you can play at both and if you get it wrong no-one is judging.

What do you remember about your screen test for the BBC?

Absolutely every single minute in detail! I arrived a trained actor heavily reliant on script and came out wondering what happened. It was a detailed whirlwind. My exit was held-up by the Queen's visit to TV Centre. I channelled it as the Queen giving my audition the Royal seal of approval. Thanks Your Maj'.

It was good to shake her hand when she visited the CBeebies studio at Salford this summer, some ten years later.

What have been your funniest moments on screen and on stage?

I have had quite a few. They are usually to do with corpsing - losing all sense of reality and finding the most benign thing funny, to such an extent of being completely unable to carry on performing the scene or link. Recently, I was in the CBeebies studio with Andy Day and Cerrie Burnell, Andy had to lie on the floor and wriggle like a worm saying 'wiggle, wiggle, wiggle'. Another time, all the presenters were in filming for Christmas and the giggles kicked in. The director was taking it far too seriously which just made it ten times worse. I guess you had to be there. One occasion, for the first time since I started my career with CBeebies, I had to leave the studio and someone else had to film the link.

On stage, I really enjoyed touring with 'The Twits' (my first big theatre job in my first year), we were in the middle of our 255th performance when someone suggested we play 'pass the pinch' whereby you could get pinched by one of the performers on stage during the show and the game was to not be left with the pinch by the end of the performance, otherwise there would be a forfeit. Something to keep the humour up and... erm great for focus and concentration..

What do your former stockbroker colleagues think of your change of career now after 10 years on Cbeebies?

They are probably thinking what a mug! He's prancing around on stage for peanuts and we're here raking in up to £1-million per year. Most of them I don't see anymore which is fine by me.

What was it like helping to launch the Cbeebies channel and what do you remember of your first appearance?

To begin with, it was just a job to get my face known on telly, I hadn't planned on staying too long. Early career opportunity and all that. There was a lot to get used to technically with a two camera shoot, a producer listening to diction and how we annunciate. Not to mention having to develop a rapid quick short-term memory for scripts as you go, working directly with the camera, sing nursery rhymes, make model toys, etc. It was tricky! But with the new channel launch we had all embarked on a new journey and I think that bought me time to settle in because everyone was trying to work it out what was to happen. When we went straight to number one children's channel it certainly helped.

What have been your personal highlights so far?

Realising I could do the job well. Playing all sorts of characters in all manner of disguises. Getting to go and see the Jools Holland Hootenanny live. Meeting the likes of icon Daley Thompson, brilliant actor David Harewood, and great musician David Grant, all black British stars - and to find that they knew who I was and were fans of what I do has been special. Keepy-uppy headers with legend John Barnes was like a dream come true. Meeting Cherie Blair at No.10 and her accepting my invitation to bring Leo to the CBeebies studio. Filming in the Masai Mara. Becoming the presenter and face of CBeebies in Africa. Running the London marathon on the channel. Never being nominated for a BAFTA. The number raps with Andy. Shaking hands with the Queen and meeting and filming in the pool with Rebecca Adlington have all been great highlights.

Can you tell me more about your stage show tour?

It's called 'Sid's Show' and is an exciting, energetic 55mins show for families with 3-7 yr olds containing new music, songs, interactivity, magic and bundles of fun. Set off on a journey to help Sid find his shoes and socks, meeting some lovely characters whilst venturing on the quest. Sid's Show is touring the UK - we have just added Dunfermline for the end of January with dates going well into 2013. It will knock your socks off! Go to **facebook.com/sidsloane** or **www.sidsloane.org** for tour dates and to book tickets.

Sid Sloane

JOHN SPARKES

PEPPA PIG, FIREMAN SAM, SHAUN THE SHEEP, THE BIG KNIGHTS,
BEN & HOLLY & LITTLE KINGDOM,

A personal comedy hero of mine! The man behind Naked Video's Siadwel, Absolutely's deliciously crude Frank Hovis and BAFTA winning Barry Welsh also lends his vocal talents to a number of more recent children's favourites – Fireman Sam, Shaun the Sheep and Peppa Pig. Ladies and gentlemen, pray silence please for.... Mr. Potato!

In my youth I went to drama school and did a post graduate acting course. I'd also trained as a teacher and although I'd trained as both I worked as a teacher for a while at a school, but I'd always fancied my chances at writing and performing because, even though we didn't do writing at drama school I was a big fan of Monty Python and I was always scribbling down sketches. While I was at college a couple of us got together and we'd write sketches and do reviews and people would laugh, so that was the start of it, I think it was a fairly traditional sort of way. The other people in the group got jobs so basically I was left on my own for writing and performing. I then became aware of what was then called the alternative cabaret circuit in London, mostly, so I moved to there. In those days they had an open spot at the end of the evening, a couple of people who were new could try out 5 minutes of material, for no money and if you were funny you'd get a booking to come back sometime, so I started doing those and that's how I started. I was always doing characters, such as Siadwel, Frank Hovis and Gwyn who did a ventriloquists routine with a house brick! He was the first thing I did on television on a programme called 'The Fame Game' for Granada which was the first talent show they'd done for a long time since Opportunity Knocks stopped being broadcast. It was hosted by Tim Brooke-Taylor among others and it was a mixture of the old school acts and the 'alternatives' as we were sort of known. So I did that while I was doing the stand up work and went to the Edinburgh Festival and got seen.

The reason I got booked to do Naked Video for BBC2 was because I wasn't Scottish. They'd made a series called 'Naked Radio' in Scotland just for Scottish audiences, which went down very well and they got the chance to do it on the television for the network but they were told they had to get some people in it who are not Scottish because they were all Scots, so Helen Lederer and myself got in for that reason!

That's how I got into Absolutely in a way too, but a little differently. The four Scottish guys Jack Docherty, Pete Baikie, Moray Hunter and Gordon Kennedy, know as the 'Bodgers' were Edinburgh based and they got their own radio series and when they got a second series they were told there were too many Scots and it all sounded the same and they needed to get some non-Scottish voices in there. I don't think they would tell you things like that these days but this was back in the 80s, so once again I got the job because I wasn't Scottish. I knew them anyway and knew the producer Alan Nixon because they were aware of the cabaret circuit and I'd been doing quite a lot on that and I'd already done Siadwel on Naked Video. So that's how I got my two breaks in TV by not being Scottish. It's one way in, I suppose.

John Sparkes

The way into children's television was because of Absolutely. Mark Baker and Neville Astley who created Peppa Pig liked Absolutely and came to see me and asked if I'd like to write for a series they were doing called The Big Knights for the BBC, which was for children of all ages, so it wasn't specifically aimed at children or adults, because they liked the stuff I wrote for Absolutely, so they asked if I'd do that and so I did. I did some of the voices for it but the two Big Knights were Brian Blessed and David Rintoul. That only went for one series because I think the BBC weren't quite sure how to market it because it was neither aimed at adults or children, it was a bit like Shaun the Sheep now in that children of all ages can enjoy it. But Mark and Neville continued to work and created a pilot for Peppa Pig, so I did the narrator for that and Morwenna Banks – another one from Absolutely - was also doing it and we just stayed with them. Since then Mark has said I've been in everything they've done, either as a writer or a performer. They also did a one-off animated film called 'Jolly Roger' which was nominated for an Oscar. It didn't win, but I was the Captain Jolly Roger. I then did voices for Ben and Holly's Little Kingdom which is the latest thing they've been doing.

It was because of Absolutely that I got to do Shaun the Sheep as well because the people behind it was aware of the programme, I think everyone was of that generation when we were on the telly. They got in touch and did a reading for them and heard nothing for a long time and thought they must have cast someone else, but lo and behold about 18 months later I got a call to say 'can I come down to Bristol because we're going to record some now' because it takes a long time for that sort of animation.

Shaun the Sheep, unlike all the other animated things, is in post production when I come in. There's no dialogue deliberately so they haven't got to re-voice it to sell it to other countries, it's all sorts of sounds, so the farmer does a lot of muttering and mumbling and never actually says anything you can distinguish as words, in fact, if I do sometimes say a word they say 'John, can you do that again, it sounded a bit like 'b*llocks'" so we'd re-do that. I'm actually post-synching it, which is quite tricky because you have to try and match the lip synch and the expression on the face and you don't have any words to say, just noises, so it's quite a challenging job, for me anyway. Justin Fletcher (Mr. Tumble) does the voice for 'Shaun the Sheep' and they auditioned high and low to get the right voice, loads and loads of people, members of staff at Aardman as well as actors, then they got to Justin and he got it in one. He's really very very good.

The original plan for 'Shaun the Sheep' was that they weren't going to have any voices for any of the characters, but when they played it they found it just needed something as it was a bit quiet, so they decided to put some sounds in at least. It's like a silent comedy in a way, but it was a bit *too* silent at first.

A pig from Shaun the Sheep

We always leave the pigs to last because their squeals are quite a strain on the voice. Because there are three of them I have to do all of the sounds three times and they mix it together. The pigs are usually quite excited or angry about something so there's quite a lot of high pitched squealing so the voice is a bit ragged after doing that so we leave it until the end of the session.

'Fireman Sam' happened in the same way, they knew my work from 'Absolutely' and knew I did voices and lots of different characters, so they got me down to Cardiff. That was done with a script and it was animated to make the characters faces fit the words we'd already recorded – the easier way.

I don't voice 'Fireman Sam' now. The original 'Fireman Sam' was done by John Alderton and they reinstated him many many years later and then got more characters in as well. Originally they tried me to do every single character but I just couldn't get enough differentiation between the four children so they had to get two actresses Joanna Ruiz and Sarah Hadland who did three of the children and I was left doing Naughty Norman.

The charm of these things are because they are slow and low tech and there's almost a feeling you could do it yourself. If you've watched enough episodes of 'Blue Peter' you'd know how to make your own models and figures. I used to like things like 'The Clangers'. It was pretty weird when you think about it, but that was part of the joy.

Three or four years ago there was a national tour of 'Fireman Sam' and the actors were in full body costumes, poor sods, and I voiced all the characters I did for them, so these poor actors were miming to the dialogue I'd recorded. It must have been a warm job. My first job as an actor was in a rabbit skin as a magician's assistant. When they were starting the sci-fi sitcom 'Red Dwarf', Rob and Doug the writers, again new me from 'Absolutely' and they got me to audition for Kryten and thank god I didn't get it, because Robert Llewellyn, who played Kryten in the end would get an ear infection at the end of every series because he got so hot and sweaty in the costume. So I was relieved really.

All credit to Mark and Neville for what they've done with 'Peppa Pig' because they're very hands on and extremely careful about any of the merchandise. There's a 'Peppa Pi'g theme park now and they were involved in the planning and designing of that which I think is very good. They didn't just say, 'yeah yeah, give us the money' and did what they like, they were very particular about keeping that 'Peppa Pig' ethos. It's nice. It has a very charming, homely feel about the whole thing and it's safe. I think that's one of the reasons why parents generally accept their children watching 'Peppa Pig', as these things go, if parents don't mind their children watching television then, for young children, Peppa Pig's probably seen as a good thing.

One of the writers for 'Peppa Pig' was saying (and I think he was half joking) that he was getting a bit of stick from the other dads that he plays football with where he lives because the father in Peppa Pig is cast as a bit of a buffoon really, his DIY efforts usually fail and Mummy Pig is the clever one who's working away and Daddy Pig is a bit menial. They say that he's giving men a bad name here, but he'd say 'Oh, f**k off, it's just a bit of fun, you idiot.'

They've made 4 series and 208 episodes so far and over the years they have introduced more supporting characters such as Mr. Labrador (I mention him because I do his voice and sounds a bit like Tommy Cooper) Pedro Pony's father (who mysteriously sounds a little bit like Sean Connery) Mr. Wolf and Mr. Fox who's a bit of a wide boy, but my favourite is Mr. Potato who is the most surreal because all the others are animals at least, whereas Mr. Potato, I think we can agree, is a vegetable, but even so, he's animate and has some sort of intelligence and speaks and for no reason, well, no good reason, has this outrageous French accent. Again this is to Mark and Neville's credit that they asked me to try a few voices for this new character and because I like to muck about and do extreme things like that, they said 'yep, that's funny, we'll go with that'. Why should a potato have a French accent? I can't think of a reason really unless you're making a programme in France, but Mr. Potato seems to be quite popular.

A couple of weeks ago there was the Thames Festival on the South Bank and BAFTA had arranged for a session where they'd be screening 'Peppa Pig', 'Little Kingdom' and 'The Big Knights' with a question and answer section as well, so there was Mark and Neville, the mums and dads, Morwenna was there and Daddy Pig and we'd come up and answer questions and I was asked what characters I do, so I said I was the narrator and that I was Mr. Potato too and they were delighted! So was I, because he doesn't crop up very much, but that was a good thing because Mr. Potato is a vegetable and he has his vegetable theme park – Wonderful World of Vegetables, so we want to encourage children to like vegetables.

I think all actors like voice overs, because you don't have to learn the words. You've got the pleasure of saying them and then you go home while everybody else has got to deal with the editing and the writing. It's a great job!

My characters such as Siadwel and Frank Hovis aren't based on real people - what a knightmarish world it would be if they were. They kind of arose from mucking about doing different voices at home, because my own voice is basically, pretty ordinary, so any comedy done in my own voice would be less rich than something done with a characters voice, as there's a suggestion that they've got a more interesting life and lived more at the extremes one way or the other, Frank Hovis certainly. The only character who was based very loosely on anyone was DIY enthusiast Denzil from Absolutely. My next door neighbour was Welsh and very keen on DIY and did have 3 sheds in his garden which were full of DIY tools - he could have built another shed if he wanted to - and he did have this kind of slightly strangulated Welsh voice, so Denzil was very loosely based on him.

I suppose they're types of people. Frank is a sort of northern club comic, probably an amalgam of several northern club comics but not deliberately so. I was just aware there was a type of person who was like that but it was just my general purpose impression of that kind of person but nobody in particular. I'm not particularly good at copying real people anyway.

I think I was 16 when I saw my first Monty Python and I've been very very influenced by that, as a lot of people were and I also really love Peter Cook and Dudley Moore and Derek & Clive later on. Not so much stand up comedians though. I didn't really see any. I was in Swansea in the 1960s and there were no comedy clubs, the only kind of live comedy would be the club comics but I don't think I was even aware of such a thing. If the careers advisor at school suggested going into comedy as a career I would have thought him insane. He would have thought me insane for thinking such a thing because people didn't do it. There's a lot of comedy now but there wasn't in those days. It was after the likes of Python, Oxbridge, Pete & Dud, and the alternative comedians Rik Mayall and Alexei Sayle hit the scene that people started to realise that you could actually make quite a decent living doing comedy and I think once the word got out then all sorts of people were having a go. There's just so much of it now, it's astonishing.

I've picked up a few Welsh BAFTA's and they were mainly for a series called 'Barry Welsh is Coming'. Barry Welsh is the anchor man, sat at a desk and he'd go to various different items within the show. For the first series he did some interviews, ones with an actor playing a character, which was scripted and other interviews with real people, such as Glenys Kinnock, so it was a bit like Mrs. Merton, but not as good as her, by quite a long way, but we dropped that for the second series and stuck to scripted stuff. I think the best thing in the programme was Hugh Pugh, who was a roving reporter for a segment called 'Look Out Wales' and the idea was that he would be reporting from different part of Wales but what happened each week is that he reports from Fishguard, where he lives. He has a very angry relationship with Barry Welsh and he hates him and Barry Welsh is rather scared of Hugh Pugh. Both characters are me and through the miracle of television we have them talking with each other. What I like about Hugh Pugh is that it's a mixture of me and archive footage. We discovered that ITV Wales, or HTV as they were then, had this gigantic archive of current affairs and news footage going right back to the 50s, but we started picking up from the 60s. Usually when people are being interviewed they're usually quite cross about something, that's why they're being interviewed – 'so what do you think about these plans to build a factory in your back garden?' - so these very angry people were giving their answers but Hugh Pugh would be asking a completely different question, so therein lies the comedy. We got the idea from Steve Martin's film 'Dead Men Don't Wear Plaid' who used old film noir footage whereas we used old regional news footage. All of these characters lived in Fishguard too. Two of those BAFTAs were for Hugh Pugh Specials, 'Fishguard Film Festival' and "Hugh Pugh's History of Wales" and the other two were for Barry Welsh programmes.

We did all those segments in black and white and the main reason for this is that the older footage was in black and white and the more recent stuff was in colour and because we were cutting so many pieces together, we couldn't constantly keep going from black and white to colour and back again, so we made the whole thing monochrome, including Hugh Pugh and explained this by saying in Fishguard everything IS in black and white, Fishguard has not gone into colour yet. From time to time Barry Welsh would comment on this and Hugh Pugh would berate him for being racist – 'what's wrong with black and white? Have you got something against it?' It had that slightly in the past quality, which I like very much. I do find the modern world a little bit too modern sometimes!

I also had an old man character called Mr. Ffff. I did an old man in 'Absolutely', Bert Bastard so I just have an affinity for old men as I'm rapidly becoming one. There was always two sides, the filthy material – which was old Mr. Ffff, Bert and Frank Hovis and then there was the very surreal side which was Siadwel, Denzil and Hugh Pugh a bit too.

I also did a series for BBC Wales called 'Pub Quiz' which was hosted by Frank Hovis. I watched it back and even I was astonished about how filthy it was. I was writing with John Irwin and we made 20 programmes and did them all in one go, with just the two of us writing it. Filth is relatively easy to write so there were quite a lot of filthy gags, but when you see them all together it was just a stream of filth. It wasn't ALL filth, but even I was astonished at the level of rudeness. I don't think BBC Wales realised what they were getting because they never came to a studio recording, so it was their own fault. They paid for it, and paid handsomely too, so they used it and it did well but they didn't recommission it, and I'm not really surprised. There were some good gags in there. John Irwin and myself can write a good dirty gag, but there was just so much of it.

I like a good, well written filthy joke. Most of them with Frank were worked into a story, there was one monologue about him basically sh*tting himself in the back of a taxi, which is absolutely hideous but there was a story to it. I'd just think of a line that made me laugh and then eventually I see how I could turn it into a story as there were a few more things that seemed to be about the same sort of thing so then I'd put them together and looked for material like that, so Frank was in the taxi battling with life, as usual.

I'm going back to doing live performances and I did my first live one for a very long time doing Siadwel. It went ok, but nobody there new him as my audience for Siadwel are in their forties. My agent was saying 'don't do the comedy clubs as know one will know who you are, just write the best hour of material you can and we'll put you out.' So I'm trying out bits of stuff in front of a live audience and, cor blimey it's terrifying! I'd forgotten how scary it is.

So watch out for Siadwel. He's been in prison all these years. He was found guilty of every crime committed in Swansea over the previous 50 years. Well, that's typically Siadwel, but he's out now and can be seen again!

John Sparkes

Mr Potato

SUSAN STRANKS
MAGPIE, PAPERPLAY

Susan hit our TV screens as one of the original presenters of Blue Peter's rival programme Magpie. She then went on to create and present Paperplay alongside the fluffy spider duo Itsy & Bitsy. Since then Susan has been an enthusiastic and determined children's radio campaigner, but her first day on Magpie proved to be an explosive event!

I started as an actress when I was 9 and was in the original version of the film 'The Blue Lagoon'. I played Jean Simmon's character as a little girl. We went off to Fiji for 9 weeks to film and it was incredible for me. I was supposed to have a tutor but I don't remember being tutored much, I was trying to climb coconut trees and dive for shells and things like that. Then I went onto do another couple of films, one was with the wonderful David Lean, I had a little part in his film 'Madeleine', not one of his best ones but it was wonderful working with him and he's an incredible man. Then my parents thought I getting very spoiled and they thought I ought to give it up and go back to school, so I did and when I left school I went to RADA and had a stint as a member of the panel on Juke Box Jury. While at RADA I met Robin Ray, whom I later married.

After I left RADA I had some bits and pieces of work in repertory, film and TV including a period in Emergency Ward 10, then Robin and I were offered the opportunity of working for six months in Michigan US in repertory doing Brecht, Shaw and Shakespeare - he as director and I as an actor in an Anglo American company.

On our return, I auditioned for 'Magpie'. It was going to be a rival for 'Blue Pete'r and at first they wanted a husband and wife team because the producer, a wonderful girl called Sue Turner, who's no longer with us, had been to one of the Scandinavian countries and seen a successful husband and wife team doing the kind of magazine programme they wanted, so they approached my husband, Robin and I but Robin was involved with something else at the time but I said I'd love to audition, not feeling for a minute I'd get it, so I auditioned and did silly things like standing on my head and other impromptu things and I got it, which was lovely. I worked alongside Pete Brady, who's Canadian and had done quite a lot of work in television and Tony Bastable who, thankfully, was very experienced because I'd only doing acting work and never any talking to the camera. Tony was brilliant at talking off the cuff and I learned a tremendous amount from him – and it went on for six years.

The very first edition of Magpie was an interesting one because one of the tasks I'd been set was to go into a balloon race in Sussex and in those days they were Hydrogen balloons. It was very exciting. It was a very clear day and quite windy too. There was this wonderfully old fashioned, beautifully made basket with leather padding all around the edges. It was going to be a race and I think there were about 7 of us in the basket which was quite a lot. I thought I'd better dress warm because the wind will be cold up there, quite forgetting that, of course, you go along with the wind so you don't feel the wind or the cold at all. I think I had a sound box across my shoulders because we used mobile sound recording equipment and I was carrying it with me because it wasn't as easy as it is now. We went up, all of us standing and it was fine but there was one woman with us who was a member of the public who started to panic and was getting quite hysterical when she realised she didn't like heights when she got up there. The man skippering the balloon was called Anthony Smith, who was a completely eccentric wild Englishman, known to be quite daredevil, but he seemed to cope alright and he sat her down and for the whole of the flight she was sitting in the bottom of the basket. The flight continued and I was giving my commentary of it, saying how wonderful it was, we must have been up there for 30-45 minutes with various balloons all around us taking part in this race, then the time came for us to come down so we started to descend and you never quite know where you're going to come down because it can be a bit hit and miss and so we were aiming for this farmers field. The descent was fine, the woman who was hysterical was sitting quite quietly in the bottom of the basket and the cameraman was doing his work and I was commentating on the descent, then we landed in the field and the wind, as it does, started pulling the balloon along away from the basket, just along the ground while it settles, and all of a sudden the thing blew up! An absolutely huge explosion of fire. Thank God it was some distance away from the basket. I was knocked out for a split second. Everybody else had leapt out of the balloon and ran to hide behind a nearby hedge. When I came to, I was very very frightened, obviously, and there was still flames coming out of the balloon and I leapt out of the basket and ran towards where the others were and eventually they got it under control, but I had cut my lip, I think I hit it against the equipment that I was carrying and I had to have two stitches in it – I've still got a tiny tiny scar on my lips to show for it – and that was my first day on Magpie! They said they thought it was sparked by a farmer who was smoking his pipe nearby!

I always used to think 'Blue Peter' was an extremely good show but it was seen by the audience then as slightly more safe and more 'mumsy' and the presenters at that time, although it did change, were seen more like aunts and uncles rather than sisters or brothers. We were considered rather racier and I think a lot of children weren't allowed to watch us, because I think we represented something a bit too racey and off-the-wall for them. Our audience did build and we had features like 'Puff the Pony' which were quite proper and English, but we also had more pop stars and I think some of the items we did were a little bit more off-the-wall than the things that 'Blue Peter' did and I definitely think we were a rival to them.

I did some wonderful things on 'Magpie', I went gliding which was very exciting. It was so quiet and a lovely way to see the countryside. They always used to get us to do exciting things and I loved it. My dad always used to say to me 'you like everything by turns and nothing long' which exactly encapsulates my life and what I like.

'Paperplay' was something I created that I pitched to the bosses. They desperately wanted me to stay on 'Magpie', they even offered me the production of it, but I left because I started to feel stale. Before I was able to say with great enthusiasm to my young audience - I've never done this before, let's do this together – and we found that items were coming around again and we were doing similar sorts of things and I said I really didn't feel as fresh as I was. They asked me to produce it and, I suppose, I should have had a go at it but I didn't really want to produce my fellow presenters and I thought it was time to move on to other things, I'd had a lovely stint. I suppose it was the best job of my life, it suited me perfectly.

I loved doing 'Paperplay' with Charles Warren, who was another very good producer and director at that time at Thames TV. There was a lot of talent at Thames when it started and probably still is, what remains of it! It was full of very exciting, interesting people who were very keen to make it all work and it was very successful as a brand. It was fun to do. I wanted to make a series of programmes for little children rather like what I'd done on Magpie but simpler things, making things out of normal throwaway household objects was the basis behind it. Norman Beardsley created Itsy and Bitsy. He was actually a studio cleaner and he was very clever with paper and used to make paper sculptures, and I think he'd done something for 'Magpie' if my memory serves, and he came to me one day with a little suitcase which he opened up and said 'what do you think of these?' and there were Itsy and Bitsy, two little finger puppet spiders. He showed me them and I asked him if he would be interested in using them in a show I was putting together. I decided there and then to include them in the show, having them help, and the squeaking and squawking, made using a swozzle, was fun, it was rather like 'The Clangers' - the children seemed to know what they were saying – and so we incorporated them. Norman made a lot of the paper sculptures that surrounded the set and we made the things together. He was very clever and his paper sculptures were lovely and Itsy and Bitsy were a very cute idea and I thought well worth putting on telly.

Towards the end of 'Paperplay' I was heavily pregnant. I was also doing a programme about film for the BBC with a producer who's no longer with us, called John Buttery, and I worked up to the very last day. One of the Paperplays on YouTube has got me in a sort of Indian print smock dress and I was very pregnant then and I worked right up until virtually the day before my son, Rupert, was born. I thought at the time I would have my baby and have a few weeks out and then I'll go back. I wanted to go back, but then, when he arrived, I suddenly thought that I didn't want to go back into that kind of work, I'd rather stay home with him for a bit and that's how it happened. I gradually drifted out of it. I wrote a couple of poetry books and 'How to' books and then gradually got into this campaign for radio. I did a few bits and pieces but I didn't want to go back into what I called 'full time' television.

After I left 'Magpie' I was offered Sue Lawley's job on Nationwide because she was leaving to have a baby. It was a wonderful job to be offered, but I turned it down because I didn't want a desk job, I didn't trust myself to only ask the politicians what I was allowed to ask them. I'm not a journalist by profession and Sue is and is wonderful at her work. They created a strand for me called 'Down Memory Lane' that I did with Bob Wellings which I loved doing because I love history and it was about ration books and the 1940s, exactly the sort of job I wanted, but, because it was a news centred programme the slot for 'Down Memory Lane' kept being squeezed. Every time we prepared it they'd say at the last minute some politician had resigned or something like that and we've got to knock minutes off you, and it just didn't sit well in what was essentially a news programme, so I said that I didn't really want to keep doing this, it doesn't work and really doesn't feel right and Bob felt the same. It had to be too flexible and if you're trying to do a really good item it's got to be structured and it's got to be allowed to sit. Funnily enough they do it more in some of the news magazine programmes, they do have time out for a musician etc – the sort of thing 'Down Memory Lane' was doing.

'Blue Peter' never tried to poach me, I think we were seen as very different sides of the fence probably, but they did change their image, they brought in Leslie Judd who had been a dancer and they started to be more sisterly and brotherly and slightly less staid and wore clothes that were more of the days fashion so I think Magpie had some influence on them, but I'm full of admiration for what Biddy Baxter did and it's still going strong.

I've been campaigning for over 30 years for a national children's radio network. I believe radio is equally, if not more important for young children than television but the BBC will not listen and last year they ditched all their children's radio and recreated or rebranded it as 'family listening' and we get less children's radio than Children's Hour provided in the 1940s when the Home Service was the only available platform and now we've got thousands and thousands of stations and the BBC does 1 hour a day for families. What they do is like a Woman's Hour with a children's story tacked on at the end, it's appalling.

I recently received an award from the ACA (Action for Children's Arts) which is a big organisation about bringing the Arts to children and because of my efforts in radio they gave me a little award. Baroness Floella Benjamin received the JM Barrie Award and it's nice to be recognised. Vicky Ireland who runs the Polka Theatre for children is one of the directors, it's a good organisation for children's arts, quite feisty and a high pressure group. There are a lot of lovely people out there that have kids at heart and this is really the point I've been trying to make for so long and all these problems at the BBC with Savile really puts it into perspective – unless you have a policy that puts children at the centre of things, we all suffer. You have to put them first in public policy not falling off the edges and this is why I think this radio thing that the BBC has done is so appalling. One of the excuses they got for cutting children's radio was, and you won't believe it, 'perhaps todays children can no longer listen without visual stimulation' My blood runs cold when I hear it, because who's fault is that? They don't understand children any more. The children weren't listening to the paltry programmes they put on because they were patronising and not good. They don't understand how to make children's radio any more. Yes, they've got some wonderful archive stories, they have made some beautiful stuff in the past, but they've never really promoted it properly, no one even knew there was children's radio when they took it off, it was hidden away in adult speech stations.

Because I care so much I launched Abracadabra Radio in 2001 on a digital station in London, it was the world's first digital radio station for children, then I couldn't afford to stay on digital because it costs so much and I wasn't getting any revenue and I relaunched on the internet, so I now run Abracadabra as a non-profit internet station really to demonstrate what can be done while we continue the campaign.

Susan Stranks

For more information about what the campaign wants to achieve and its supporters please visit www.sound-start.com

To listen to lots of stories, songs and fun and games aimed at young children please visit www.abracadabraradio.com

HACKER T. DOG
CBBC, HACKER TIME, SCOOP

Hacker is from Wigan. Which is quite surprising really as he doesn't really mention it that much! He's also quite partial to meat paste and has a penchant for Sue Barker. I recently had some Hacker time with the face of CBBC and had an entertaining chat with him on the 'dog and bone' and it went a little something like this.

GV: What was it like for a young pup growing up in Wigan?

Hacker: It's great because I'm from Wigan and I love it here in Wigan. It's always sunny in Wigan and it's full of top notch shops where you can go out and buy all your favourite meat paste. I like beef paste best and I like it on a sandwich and I like a milky brew to wash it down.

GV: So Wigan meets all your needs then?

Hacker: Yeah meets all my needs... that's funny! that's a joke! Ha. If you spell it like 'meat'. It works.

GV: What do you really think of Dodge?

Hacker: He's my half brother, we're very close. He's from East London and I'm from Wigan. We've got a very tall mum.

GV: Do you share the same father?

Hacker: We share the same dog bowl, that's as far as it goes.

GV: As you're working in the CBBC office is there still a smell of gopher there?

Hacker: There is a slight whiff of gopher, even though we've moved from London to Salford and the waft still followed us a bit.

GV: Away from the cameras do you have a kennel or a winnebago?

Hacker: I've got a kennel in Wigan and one in the CBBC office. I have my very own garden with a picket fence round it and I love that, and then people come round and leave little gifts for me. That's because I'm dead famous you see. Fan mail and that. I've got a lot of showbiz chums you know?

GV: Such as?

Hacker: Shaun Williamson, who was Barry in Eastenders. He's my friend. Sue Barker. She begrudgingly became my friend after hounding her for 4 years at Wimbledon. I've also met Her Majesty The Queen. You know, her off the stamps?

GV: Yes.

Hacker: I met the Queen.

GV: She's very good on coins as well.

Hacker: She always looks to the left on all the photos of her on coins and the stamps.

GV: Did she look to the left when you met her as well?

Hacker: She looked to the left when she was leaving because that's where the exit was.

GV: Is there anyone else you'd like to meet?

Hacker: Yeah, I'd like to meet......I've met some more famous people you know? I've met JLS you know? They're good. Alan, the little one, Alan, he's my favourite one. I'd like to meet One Direction. I like Neil. Neil's good. Neil Styles, he's the best one.

I've met Terry Wogan and that woman Jenny Metcalfe from Hollyoaks, I've met her. Pollyanna from t' Gadget Show, she's good. I've met everyone. I'm dead showbiz. I 'ang about in those sort of circles. Tied up outside when they nip in, I'm not allowed in sometimes.

GV: If you had the chance to go on a date with Sue Barker where would you take her?

Hacker: I'd take her to a local patisserie because I like a patisserie, Sue likes a brasserie. Now, this is funny, I was talking to Sue and I said 'Oh, Sue. Sue Barker. I've met the Queen', and Sue said 'Oh, well I have lunch with the Queen on a regular basis' so I was a little bit out of sorts with Sue because she's more of a success than I am.

GV: Well, we can't be having that.

Hacker: That's what I thought, so I finished filming the episode of Hacker Time and I sent her on her merry way. I didn't hold up the shoot because I'm a professional. So I finished the show, because that's what I do. You've seen me on telly, I'm dead professional.

GV: When you went to Wimbledon did you end up chewing many of the tennis balls?

Hacker: Yes, they were furious actually. They sent me a small invoice afterwards because I dribbled on some of the tennis balls and I tinkered with Andrew Castle's bat and he was furious. I annoyed him because I called it a bat.

GV: What about Tim Henman?

Hacker: I had a photograph with him. I know Alesha Dixon from television as well. She's good.

GV: Have you done any Strictly Come Dancing yet?

Hacker: No, but I did dance for her on her show for CBBC called Alesha's Street Dance, so me and Dodge did a little dance for her and she thought it was great and she put us through. It was called "K-9".

GV: Is that because you're a dog?

Hacker: I think so, yeah, because I'm not a Doctor Who fan so it must be the dog thing.

GV: What's been the highlight of living in Wigan?

Hacker: Well, I turned the Wigan Christmas lights on you know the other night, (Ha Ha they were HIGH lights, do you get it?) with my new showbiz chum Kye from the X-Factor. He was good. He has eyeliner. He calls it Kye-liner. It's a good marketing tool for future earnings when his singing dries up.

GV: You've been in Scoop and you have your own show Hacker Time now...

Hacker: Yeah, I've done 3 series of Scoop and 2 series of Hacker Time. I've got very little memory of the first series of Scoop, I don't know what was wrong with me there, I think I must have been nervous or something. The viewers started watching more in series 2 and that's when I got all my fantastic award nominations, for I've been nominated for a BAFTA. Twice! On two separate occasions, so that's how showbiz I am. It's not bad for a little dog, is it?

GV: It's more than I've ever done.

Hacker: Well, I'm better than you.

GV: Is there any possibility of a world tour perhaps? Is Hollywood beckoning?

Hacker: Hollywood? Well Broadway, I think, is on the cards. But I don't mean Broadway in America. Broadway is a street in Wigan. But I could end up on Broadway and it wouldn't be a lie.

I'll sort of use that in my autobiography which I will probably do in a couple of years when I'm ready to retire from showbusiness.

GV: I've spoken with Phil Fletcher, what do you think about him?

Hacker: I don't know. I don't know who you're talking about. I haven't a clue. Is he the one that carries my stuff about? I won't speak to people like that. I won't speak to people who are beneath me!

GV: OK! A couple of final questions. Have you ever met Justin Bieber?

Hacker: I like his hair, he's got good hair him. Baby baby baby ooooh, baby baby baby ooooh. See, I can do it. Baby baby baby ooooh. Baby baby baby oooooh. What was his next song? I've forgotten the other one. Have you recorded this?

GV: I have, yes

Hacker: Don't forget to press 'play' and 'record' at the same time otherwise this would be a waste of time, this.

GV: Is there any last message for all your fans out there?

Hacker: Hello, everyone reading this. Thank you for your continued support for my showbusiness, top notch career. Not bad for a little dog from Wigan, eh?

Hacker T. Dog

DAVID TATE

CROC - EMU'S ALL LIVE PINK WINDMILL SHOW, GROTBAGS

As Grotbags' hapless sidekick, Croc knew only too well what it was like being on the end of her bezazer, but for David it was a role that he didn't expect to last so long but it was a time filled with fun, laughter and the occasional expletive!

I started off as a dancer when I was 18 and I got my first job at the London Palladium with 'Bruce Forsyth and the Second Generation' who were a popular song and dance group back then. I went on to do other things with the 'Second Generation' and we were lucky enough to work with a lot of celebrities of the time. There then came a time when work began to dry up and I found myself out of work, then I received a call from a good friend of mine, who also happened to be the Choreographer of the Rod Hull children's TV shows, 'The Pink Windmill Show' and 'Emu's Wide World.' In the very first series there was a guy called Freddie Stevens who was the original Croc but he was a frustrated actor that wanted to be seen and he said that he didn't want to do another series unless they could see his face, so that's when they decided to get rid of Croc and introduced this robot tin can 'Robot Redford.'

After a while, Christmas time came and the producer thought it would be fun to bring Croc back because he was so popular with the kids and wanted to see how he would work with the robot and the famous green witch Grotbags to see how the three of them worked together, so he asked me if I wanted to play Croc and I said that I didn't want to get in a skin because I was a dancer so he said to me "Oh, you're always moaning. You're out of work at the moment anyway, it's only for 3 weeks over Christmas and no one would see you" so I said I'd do it. So I got into this hot skin and just went over the top with my performance because nobody could see who I was but after that the producer, Louis Rudd and the director, Colin Clews, came down afterwards and said "I'd like you to do a series, the chemistry between the three of you works really well" and I looked up and thought "Oh no!" I didn't want to do this, but then I thought it's easy work, it's three days a week and I can continue with my dancing career and so I ended up playing Croc for another three or four years. It just worked fantastically, but after four years I must admit I got tired of working in a skin as it got so hot. In my last year, television variety was changing, they wouldn't make shows like that now because they're just too expensive, but all those times working with Grotbags and them all was like being with more children, it was one of the fun times of my life, it was fantastic.

Rod was always a prankster. He was quite a drinker, bless him, and liked his brandy and he would sometimes go around with a cigarette lighter holding it near some of the crews bums until they screamed, then they would realise he was actually burning their arse! He thought this was hysterical but, of course, they didn't.

Carol, (Grotbags the green witch) was one of the most fun loving people you could ever meet. Little kids were scared of her but that was just her character, but she was so much fun and we could ad-lib from time to time. I remember one time in the show Grotbags had to faint and collapse on to the studio floor. There is a shot of me giving her a good kick and saying... "Leave her there, she can suffer" whilst me and robot tried to escape and get away from her and the kids loved it.

Croc's skin was so hot I was almost naked inside it and I had them make me a belt with pockets that I could wear that had ice packs in it to keep me cool. One of the funniest times was when we were hanging around doing shots and one season they decided to go out live which meant that you couldn't mess about and couldn't do any lines again, so, there we were, doing a live show and I'd completely forgot. We'd not been doing live shows for so many years and suddenly we were live, then one of my ice packs burst and all the icy liquid went around my privates and I screamed "F*CK!" Thankfully nobody knew where this came from because they couldn't see my mouth, but it was a live show so that word went out across the nation, but only because poor Croc had ice all around his privates, so I got away with it because I didn't own up to it!

I sort of gave up dancing because I wanted to do more and did some writing, and have had a spiritual self help book published. I got out of the scene for a while and went soul-searching. I went to live in America for 12 years. I was a bartender in a pub called "The Londoner" in Dallas and an English girl visited the pub, she was an au-pair and home sick and she was amazed when she found out I used to be Croc as she remembered the show.

Then I got into song writing, I had some song and dance tracks produced but nothing major. I'm still writing and writing songs. I've written a musical that I'm trying to sell, so I'm keeping my toes in the business by working as a dresser on the musical Matilda which is all about children, and is a fun children's show. I seem to be drawn towards children. I think it's in my destiny!"

David Tate

BRIAN TRUEMAN

DANGERMOUSE, SCREEN TEST, COUNT DUCKULA, CHORLTON & THE
WHEELIES, JAMIE & THE MAGIC TORCH, COCKLESHELL BAY

*Brian was a close collaborator with the Cosgrove Hall animation studio writing
many of their fondly remembered shows such as Dangermouse, Jamie and the
Magic Torch, Chortton and the Wheelies and Cockleshell Bay as well as using
his vocal talents either as a narrator or giving a voice to the likes of Nanny in
Count Duckula or Stiletto in Dangermouse and not forgetting a stint he had
presenting the children's quiz Screen Test at a time when a future Oscar
winner won their film competition...*

Looking back – and it takes binoculars – on my career in...er...'showbiz', - let
alone finding myself a 'legend', I have to wonder how I got to where I am from
where I started. Certainly, the back streets of Moss Side, Manchester weren't the
most likely launch pad. I guess the answer has to be with a lot of luck and a lot
of love...

Through no fault of their own, my parents and Baby Brian had had to move in
with my mother's parents which meant that the terraced two up and two down,
donkey-stoned step, back yard and outside toilet was shared by Granny and
Grandad, Mum and Dad, Uncle Joe, me and the dog. First rung on the ladder of
luck was that my parents, despite having finished school at 14, were aspirational
working-class and desperate to escape. So, five years later and with only
shadowy memories of my first home, the three of us were in a better terraced
house in Chorlton-cum-Hardy. It even had a bathroom! And life was good; I was
loved and cared for, I had parents who tried to push me up in the world, who
made sure that I could read and, in particular, a father who loved words, loved
juggling and joking with them and loved 'acting the goat'. So far, so good.
Then, when I was about seven and a half, I started getting stomach pains and
having to have time off school. Just before my 8th birthday, I was taken into
hospital and diagnosed as having intestinal TB. With antibiotics still a miracle
waiting to happen, it was a potentially fatal disease. I was shipped off to North
Wales, to the Abergele TB sanatorium and didn't come home again until just
before I was 10. By then, my own auto-immune system had seen off the TB but
for almost two years, I'd had no education at all. Coping with Year 6 (as it now
is) when my last class was Year 3 was totally bewildering and it was only
thanks, again, to my parents, that I squeezed into a grammar school as a 'Special
Case'. My other problem (as they saw it) was that while I'd gone away talking
quite 'nicely', with a soft Lancashire accent, I'd come back with 'Salfordese'

picked up from the urban poor who were a lot more likely than the well-off to collect TB. What to do?

My best friend at school before I was ill was Geoff Oldham and so he was when I came home. Come to that, we're still friends. His father was a pharmacist – so a rung or two up the social ladder from us – and he was having elocution lessons at the eccentric Longford Academy of Speech, Dance and Drama. I must ask him why, some time. So Mama and Papa signed me up for lessons and Geoff and I attended as a pair. He did the serious stuff, I did the clowning. We didn't do the 'Dance' bit. And this turned out to be another bit of luck, another rung on the 'up' ladder because the BBC (no less!) had had a change of policy and decided to give the regions a bit more autonomy. One result was that 'North Region' had its own Head of Children's Programmes in the formidable form of Nan McDonald and she decided that too much of kids' radio drama was, so to speak, about "Penelope and her Pony" and that too many 'children' were played by adults. She cast her net out among the theatre schools, voice coaches etc. and I found myself doing an audition. And I passed (though, much later, I found it was only just)! There followed three sessions of learning microphone and studio technique. And then I waited. But not for too long because at the age of 14, I got the part of 'Tubby', cook to a gang of other scouts in "The Adventures of the Plover Patrol". And I even got paid for doing it! Two guineas, even! More adventures followed, more serials, more roles. As I got older, the parts got older. I got parts in a radio comedy sit-com 'Over the Garden Wall' with Norman Evans (no-one will know; you'll have to Google it), I was in a solemn 3rd Programme (now Radio 3) drama, I joined Equity. And I hung on through school, through university (Manchester, of course) and even, now and then, when I was serving Queen and Country by acting the part of a soldier through two years of National Service (See 'Google' above).

Back in civvies, I got some work in radio comedy, did a live commercial (Gulp!), worked alongside Benny Hill as the other half of a short-lived series about a couple of naff private eyes, even got a big part in a TV drama (about an AWOL soldier) in which, for some reason, Albert Finney had a walk-on. But there were many more weeks without jobs than with and I was starting to look for other jobs in the industry when I was tipped off that the then-1-year-old Granada Television was looking for a part-time newscaster so that Bill Grundy had more time for other things. I auditioned one Monday evening. On Tuesday, at 17.50, I was the new face of the Granada in the North newscast. In black and white television with, for technical reasons, a bright green shirt and an orange face. And that, as it happened, was the first rung on a very big ladder because, among others yet unborn, it had Dangermouse waiting at the top of it.

The ladder, mind you, was just under 20 years high and and as rung followed rung, I became in turn – and sometimes all in the same week/day – newscaster, reporter, studio interviewer, documentary voice-over, Scene at 6.30 / Cinema presenter, and documentary producer / presenter. A lot of it not relevant here – except that, when I was producing documentaries, I had to talk to Granada's Graphics Department about graphics for the programmes I was making. And there, in that haven of professionalism where people seemed to know what they were doing (which was not necessarily true of the rest of us) I encountered a couple of decent blokes called Brian Cosgrove and Mark Hall. They were interested in making animated films. Granada wasn't. I think Brian C got me to do a voice-over to a short film he'd made to show them what the potential was. They still weren't interested. Brian left; Mark followed. Another talent, Bridget Appleby left to join them just up the road from GTV in a set-up called Stop-Frame Animation, part of Manchester-based Greendow Productions.

By now, 19+ years from when I joined Granada, I was soon to move on to a more freelance life. They'd asked me to jump through a well-worn hoop once too often. In the year before I left, though, Brian Cosgrove rang me and asked if I could write a pilot script for an animation series he'd invented. I could have asked why on earth he thought I might be able to but, like most actors, I just said 'yes'. And I did and it was well received and, like the intended series, it went nowhere. Pity. About a year later, I was waiting for my contract with GTV to run out so that I could have a holiday before I joined the BBC as presenter of a new current affairs show. And, out of the blue, Brian rang me again. While I wasn't looking, he, Mark Hall and the team had been snapped up by Thames TV and were now Cosgrove Hall Productions. Could I help? They were making a model animation show and couldn't find a sufficiently barmy writer. Well, that's not how he put it but it's what he meant. And we know what I said, don't we? So I did and it worked and this time it *did* take off. It was Chorlton and the Wheelies.

So how come this ability to write scripts had mysteriously arrived in the Trueman system like a happy virus? I could and can only suppose that in the 30 years of acting out all sorts of scripts I'd somehow absorbed the shape of stories, stashed away the way characters speak, learned how to put the words in the right order and in the right places for dramatic or comic effect and all the other skills that are part of script-writing. What's more, I could play the characters in my head, listen to what they were saying and write it down. Sounds barmy, I know – and probably is. More probably it came from years of happy laughing and giggling with our children and reading them Eric Thomson's Magic Roundabout books. Eric Thompson; now there was a legend!

Chorlton, narrated by Joe Lynch, came to an end and Jamie and the Magic Torch took over. I took over the voices, too. Given the mad characters in Jamie and the psychedelic design, it wasn't surprising that there were lots of rumours that the series was drug-propelled. Not so: in my case it was more likely to have been the rush of creative adrenalin when any sane person would have been sleeping instead of writing. Life on two ladders at once is like that.

Chorlton had been model animation, Jamie was drawn. The next rung was another model animation. Cockleshell Bay was an everyday story of seaside folk and as normal and gentle as Jamie had been barmy. We made five series; 65 episodes and again I did the voices: Mum, Dad, two children, Gran Routy and so on and so on and including a donkey and a seagull. Very hard on the throat!

So far, the show's had done well enough. They pleased a UK audience and that, for the team was good enough. Then, of a sudden, and while much of the Thames executives' attention was focussed on Rosemary Ann Sisson's adaptation of the children's classic The Wind in the Willows, Brian Cosgrove more or less sneaked 'Dangermouse' into the production schedules. And, crumbs chief, didn't it take off!

DM came into being when, according to him, Brian Cosgrove was doodling and found he'd drawn a mouse. Then for no good reason he gave it an eye patch...and decided it was a character worth developing. It was, in any case, he thought, time for another animated mouse that wasn't American.
Next, he came up with DM's equally famous sidekick who, he always said, was based on his brother – the night editor at the Daily Express in Manchester and supposedly looked just like Penfold. Making Dangermouse the world's greatest secret agent was a cheeky response to the James Bond movies that were around at the time. Brian asked his friend Mike Harding to take a look at it to see how it might be developed and Mike came up with some suitably crazy storylines before Brian invited me to turn them into scripts.

Penfold

I think we had about three meetings with Mike before his touring schedule with his show made it impossible to stay in touch – but he certainly helped to establish the lunacy of DM's adventures.

It's that early stage of a show's creation that generates a lot of the fun and excitement for the writer as he tries to build up his characters' personalities. I always feel that my acting work was a great help since an actor, too, has to get under the skin of the part he's playing. In this case, of course, you had drawings to look at and often test footage of the way the character moves. So, bit by bit, even when I wasn't going to playing the parts, I got a better and better idea of the way they talked, how they interacted with other characters, how they might respond to a given situation. In the end, it feels as if they're writing the scripts because, quite often, their lines come into your head before you're aware of any conscious thought process. It's an interesting phenomenon. I think it probably means, in medical terms, that you're just going off your rocker.

One way and another, though, it looked as if the team had got it right because before long, Dangermouse was being sold all around the world and even successfully invading the homeland of DM's distant great-great cousin, Mickey. Here at home, my two sons, often subjected as a test audience to listen to my reading of the scripts, found that whereas they'd had to tolerate a good deal of scorn at school because their Dad wrote soppy kid's stuff, were suddenly being approached by their tormentors saying "Wow, Trueman – your Dad writes Dangermouse!" And so it was that I saved them from a life of shame. It's not often a father earns his children's gratitude...

So why was it so succesful? Theories abound. I think it was because it didn't write down to its audience and because it believed a joke was a joke no matter who was at the receiving end. So, for little children, there was the fun of silly, colourful characters charging about and creating mayhem. Meanwhile, their older siblings were giggling at jokes for 7-8 year-olds and, naturally, the younger ones aspired to their elders' level of understanding. Meanwhile, what the 7-8 year-olds were missing were the social, political, contemporary references to things in the adult world which is why the Mums, Dads and teenagers were watching. We had a Dangermouse Fan Club at John's College, Oxford where the brains of Britain tuned into the mad mouse's tea-party. I think it might have been the equivalent of other (or the same) students taking their teddy-bears with them when they went away from home. What tends to happen these days is that the TV powers-that-be try to second guess what age group would like what with the help of child psychologists and, like as not, the legal department. But the idea that any one child can be defined by his/her age group is ridiculous; you only have to have children of your own (Ah! Well...) to know how different they can be at identical periods of their lives. Better to offer them a plateful of rich pickings so that they can take what they want and leave what they don't – but maybe have their palates tickled by what they didn't know they would fancy.

For whatever reason, DM went on and on. Even when it stopped, it started again. I think I wrote about 120 episodes, many of them in the half of the week that was left after I'd written a simultaneously-running Wind in the Willows adventure... While, however, The (apparently) One-eyed White Wonder was taking a break, one of the animators in CHP (Cosgrove Hall Productions) came up with an idea for another drawn series and Alias the Jester was born. I loved it! I loved it particularly because it was really a domestic comedy sit-com albeit in the context of a crazy interpretation of mediaeval life. And I'm quite a domestic person, very at home with close familial relationships. I'm also, like most writers, a vampire – sucking the life blood out of people I know. So King Arthur, grumpy and hen-pecked, was my father. And I played him with my father's voice and wrote him with some of my father's expressions. Queen Gertrude (voiced, as was Sir Pinkly Percival, by Jimmy Hibbert) was my step-mother but with more than a squeeze of lemon since the real thing was gushingly sentimental. And so on. It was a great hit with brilliant viewing figures. And it only ran for two series. Odd, that. The problem was that Thames TV were by then looking for investment money to help with the rising costs of production. An American broadcaster was keen to have a piece of CHP's output (the good news) but reckoned that their audience wouldn't be able to understand Alias (the bad). Subsequent work with the Americans led one to believe that they didn't think their audiences could understand anything that had more than two syllables. So, though I didn't know it at the time, the show was to be dumped. And that explains why, when, in 1986 Alias the Jester won the BAFTA award for the Best Animation Film, the mineral water flowed like champagne.

And in its place and out of his coffin, rose Duckula. Sorry, Count Duckula! Which, as it happens, turned out to be just as much fun but an even bigger hit than Alias. Directed and mostly designed by the eccentric, awkward, argumentative Chris Randall, it again contained an awful lot of family life – if the not family life as we normally know it. I hope. So, as much as the crazy plots and the extremes of animated lunacy, it was about the relationships between Duckula himself, Igor the Evil Butler and Nanny. Starring – again – as Duckula was David Jason adding another lead character to his Dangermouse and Toad from Wind in the Willows. Not to mention dozens of other voices. Indeed, just to interrupt myself, having a small cast playing lots of parts was another of the lasting characteristics of CHP's productions. Dangermouse had David Jason, Terry Scott, Edward Kelsey, Jimmy Hibbert and me (Stiletto) but I might well play half-a-dozen or more characters from Brummie caravanners to camp snakes as well as any monsters that needed a basso-profundo growl. And the same for my four fellow actors;

Nanny

and if there were 25 characters in the script, still five actors. The same principle held – with some different actors with Duckula and with Alias. So we became a tight-knit group and the performances benefitted from the instinctive interplay that developed.

Back from the interruption, Count Duckula was another hit and ran for 65 episodes. By now, since I was writing other series, too, we had three writers even if it had fallen to me to establish the style and build the detailed nature of the characters and their relationships. Which reminds me that Mark Hall, who produced the model animation side of CHP's output and liked to bring literary classics to the screen (hence Wind in the Willows: the original book and the spin-off 66-part series) had also done that with Robert Browning's poem The Pied Piper of Hamlin. And somewhere I have a newspaper cutting that credits me with writing Dangermouse, Duckula and The Pied Piper. Well, I may not be in the first flush of youth ("May not"? Come on, Brian!) but I don't think I was born in 1812.

The last series I wrote for the now CHF (F for Films instead of P for productions; don't ask me) was an adaptation of Terry Pratchett's Truckers. I'd started by writing for model animation and was to end doing the same. And I had a nice part to play as well. We were supposed to be adapting the other two books in Pratchett's trilogy but it never happened; Margaret Thatcher had intervened. Enraged by Thames TV's documentary Death on the Rock (q.v.) and seeing the opportunity to use independent

Brian Trueman

television's profits as a milch cow, she introduced the franchise system whereby the TV companies had to bid for the right to operate and hand over umpteen millions for the privilege. Thames were confident that they'd keep London weekdays – but were mistaken. As a result, they were reduced to being a programme provider for other companies and, looking for economies, the London HQ predictably decided to wield the axe on their little provincial set-up in Chorlton-cum-Hardy. Series in development were cancelled, a staff of 140 folk shrank to 70 in two weeks – and went on shrinking steadily thereafter. A time of very great sadness and hurt for many people – including the company's 'bosses' Brian Cosgrove and Mark Hall. So I was out of a job that was pretty well a life.

I went on to write for others: Budgie the Little Helicopter, some stuff for Fraggle Rock, some Thomas the Tank Engine scripts and, a real buzz of a job, writing the book and lyrics for a musical adaptation of Plautus' (Roman writer of social comedies) Miles Gloriosus which translates as the Swaggering Soldier but, for the New Shakespeare Company's production, was titled just The Swaggerer. It brought me the privilege of working with Carl Davies who wrote the music and seeing a stage show brought to hilarious life by a terrific cast. I'd have liked to do more...but it will be another lasting if one-off memory.

I do a bit of writing these days but what I miss more than anything is the acting; it's where I came from, that's what the writing developed from and that's what I'd like to get back to. I've just (August 2012) recorded a large slab of Michael Morpurgo's latest novel, A Medal for Leroy, as an audio book and that was a really enjoyable experience. I've never dreamed of writing a novel because the idea of sitting down and spending a year, say, to develop some idea (which, in any case, I don't seem to have) is quite alien to me. I have written a kids' book which Brian C. and I are working to develop as an animated ebook but very largely I've written because people have asked me to. Personally, I'm quite happy in my own skin, but professionally speaking I don't particularly want to be me, I'd rather be several other characters. If I were to write a novel I might have to look into my inner soul and those of my relatives (if they and I have got them!). Altogether too introspective. Given a job to do and the pay for doing it, I'm comfortable - maybe because it doesn't feel like self-indulgence, it feels like doing a job and I'm happy with that approach.

In the beginning it was Brian and the sadly-missed Mark who asked me to write for them. They were what's now a rare breed: people who had a real feel for 'showbiz' and an instinct for what would work on their particular stage. Not only that, but they recognised people's potential before, if I'm anything to go by, those people knew it themselves and, once they'd decided they'd got the right person for the job, gave them their trust and support and let them get on with it. I once got round to asking them why on earth they asked this TV producer / performer to write scripts for them. They thought; they pondered... and said they couldn't remember. So I shall never know but I'm awfully glad they did and I'll settle for that.

Brian Trueman

Dangermouse and
his trusty sidekick

TIM WHITNALL

MIKE & ANGELO, TELETUBBIES, FIFI AND THE FLOWERTOTS, THE BEEPS,
ROARY THE RACING CAR, TREE FU TOM

It's not every day you get to walk on ceilings but it was just your average day in the life of Tim Whitnall when he was playing the alien Angelo in CITV's long running kids sit-com Mike & Angelo. Since then Tim has lent his vocal skills to a host of other children's TV shows including the new show Tree Fu Tom. Tim is also a critically acclaimed writer having created a stage show about Eric Morecambe and a TV biopic about the late great Kenny Everett. I managed to prise Tim away from his writing long enough for an insightful Q&A.

Who was influential in your childhood, on radio/TV and in your family?

Performers that influenced me... Stanley Unwin, Elvis Presley, Muhammed Ali, Evel Knievel...

When did you first realise you had a gift for creating different voices?

In terms of any gift for performing different voices: I've honestly never though about it. My mum used to read us bedtime stories, deftly slipping into and out of character so I might have absorbed that. I remain traumatised by her wholly convincing troll so it was certainly formative. If ever I recount any of my three 'titanic-dotes' (as my other half refers to them) I find myself doing that 'Jackanory Syndrome' - thing; a condition I find irritating when other people do it, making me a card-carrying hypocrite. Many of us mimicked our teachers at one time or another but I have a vague memory of 'doing' my English teacher in front of a class, being caught red-handed and calmly being told to finish the exploration of subtext in "The Mayor Of Casterbridge" - as him.

When did you know you wanted to be a performer?

I think becoming a performer just happened, really. I had played piano and sung in school concerts - with varying degrees of success - but my debut in a professional theatre occurred at the Theatre Royal, Bury St. Edmunds in 1974 when I was called out of the audience and made to levitate on a board stretching over two chairs by a pair of rather fabulous 'drag illusionists'. And if you don't believe me, the phrase, 'Wriggle for us Timmy', still echoes through the family annals. I did wriggle and to his day have no idea how that board remained solid as they whipped the first... then the second chair away, leaving me hovering above Suffolk. But I do remember that rushing roar of the audience and heat from the lights.

Where did you learn to juggle?

Michael Benz (Mike) and I learned to juggle for Mike and Angelo. We taught ourselves from an old book. Good tip: practice over a bed, then you don't have to bend down and pick up the balls up every time you drop them. Lovely to have it as a skill but Michael smoked me every time!

What are your memories of getting the role of Angelo?

My main memory of doing my original audition for M&A (in the old Thames TV building in the Tottenham Court Road) was of the fire alarm going off during it and having to conclude my test on the pavement outside. When I got called-back for a pucker camera-test, I actually taped it on the old Rainbow set at Teddington - a personal thrill.

What did you enjoy most about your time on the show?

The whole process, I guess. I LOVED learning a show, rehearsing it, recording it,wiping the hard-drive and having to restart on a new one. We had a brilliant crew, talented directors, some fantastic guest artists - Ron Moody, Christopher Biggins, Alan Ford, Elizabeth Estensen, John Savident - to name but a few, always a very happy core cast and in writers Lee Pressman and Grant Cathro, two ring-sharp legends of Children's TV. (I was a huge fan of T-Bag!)

Are there any behind the scenes stories you can share?

Behind the scenes... I did once suffer an exquisite fracture of my left elbow when I slipped on a patch of wet floor in the hallway. Off to Kingston A&E then back to work after lunch. What a trooper.

What was your favourite episode/moment? Do you miss walking on ceilings? loved the episode with Brian Murphy where I had to play Scarlett O'Hara. I can still walk on ceilings.

What happened at the end of Mike & Angelo?

I suppose the show - like all shows - just reached the natural end of its life. I do remember the make-up artists Viv Gunzi and Sally Hennen saying to me after the final scene of the last series, 'We're shaving your head now, no more combovers!', which I shall always love them for. Apart from follical emancipation, it also spelt that Angelo and his red-tinted barnet had zoomed off into deep space and that was that - twelve series is an amazing run for any series.

Do you prefer writing, voice work or performing these days?

I write now, subsidising that with the odd V.O which is an extremely fortunate position to be in. I haven't performed on stage or TV for a few years now and I really don't miss it despite a long, varied and really enjoyable theatre career. I had always written but when I decided to dedicate myself to it, my

What are your tips for writing and getting it done?

You should know, Garry! I find personally that I tend to immerse myself in a project wholly and graft as hard as I can to make it work. You have to remain collaborative and flexible and be able to take an external view of what you've achieved. There is no substitute for getting what you've written in front of a living, breathing audience - be it a film, a TV piece or a stage-play.

Do you feel protective over your voice characters, like the fondness and love towards family members?

I suppose feeling an affection for any character you've created can happen - but not to the extent of exhibiting cardboard cut-outs of them in the loo or cuddly toys of them on my pillow! I do own a "Tree Fu Tom" key-ring though.

What was it about Eric Morecambe that inspired you to write a play about his life?

As far as the inspiration for "Morecambe" goes - it was knowing the phenomenally gifted actor Bob Golding (Eric Morecambe) who had worked with a director (Guy Masterson) at the Edinburgh Fringe. Guy had mentioned the notion of a one-man show starring the mutli-talented Mr. Golding which might bring to life 'fifty percent of Britain's best-loved double act' - a writing challenge too delicious to pass up on, with Bob playing every single character in the play - be they male or female. Our co-producer Anna Murphy got us all in to a restaurant and whipped the four of us into a collaboration which took the play to Edinburgh, into the West End and out on two tours. Eric & Ernie and Kenny Everett are my comedy heroes, along with Python, Do Not Adjust Your Set, Rutland Weekend Television, Fall and Rise Of Reginald Perrin, Steve Martin, Robin Williams, Bill Hicks...

What have been the highlights of your career so far?

Winning both Fringe First and Laurence Olivier Awards for "Morecambe"... a Writer's Guild Award Nomination for my first film "The Hide"... having my Kenny Everett biopic "Best Possible Taste" commissioned by BBC 4... getting to play my hero in the West End musical "Elvis" (my very first job)... narrating the "Teletubbies"... playing a tomato in a corporate video... I honestly have NO complaints!

Tim Whitnall

You can read more about Tim's work at www.featherproductions.com

NICK WILTON
SATURDAY SUPERSTORE, NO. 73, PLAYAWAY, FAST FORWARD,
WYSIWYG, JUSTIN'S HOUSE

It's fair to say that Nick's had a varied career. As well as Saturday morning outings as Mo the Crow his other work has taken in sandwich quizzes, scoops, double dares, alien TV and comedy vegetables. It's likely you'll have seen Nick dressed in drag on stage, naked in Gordon Ramsey's kitchen or antagonising the residents of Albert Square but I had to ask the question that's on everybody's lips: what was it like having your hand up a crow's backside?

Never mind that, you fail to mention that the rest of me was lying on the floor between Sarah Greene's legs! It was great fun being the punk crow, Mo, on Superstore. I'd turn up at about 7 on the Saturday morning, if I remember rightly, and I'd get the script for the show, which would just be a list of the items and timings - I could pretty much say what I liked. I'm not sure Mike Read liked the crows butting in all the time though; I remember once he grabbed my beak to shut me up and I just said (through clenched teeth) "I can still talk with my beak shut, you know". Ralph Steadman was on the show once and he was knocking off brilliant cartoons left, right and centre - he did me a wonderful one of Mo, that I've still got. One of the best things about Superstore was the buffet lunch they used to lay on after the show in one of the hospitality rooms! - I'm not sure if I was actually ever last to leave, but I came close a few times.

Ralph Steadman's Mo

It all started when I was at Kent University in Canterbury studying Drama and English (1975-78), and at the end of my second year I got a message in my pigeonhole from a first year student called Jamie Rix (son of Brian, the famous farceur) who wanted to put on a revue in the first term of the next year. He had been given my name as someone who might be able to come up with some funny stuff. Anyway, we met up with a few other people and started talking through some ideas and we seemed to be on the same wavelength straight away. Well, the other people (actually there might have only been one other) dropped out one by one (or just the one) leaving Jamie and me. He and his partner, Helen, had taken over a house for the following year, so we got together through the summer and wrote the show, and I talked myself into a room in the house for my final year.

We did the show, 'Turn Off (TV Revued)', which was a huge success (well, we thought so anyway) and the Student Union said they'd give us some money to take it up to Edinburgh. But it was my final year and I went off to do other stuff - serious, ground-breaking work like being a Bluecoat for the summer at Blean Sands (Weston super Mare). I then somehow drifted into stage management for a year and a bit, thinking it was a good route to becoming a director, which at that time was my ambition.

A younger Nick

It was only after a fall from a ladder when working at the Chester Gateway theatre that I moved back to London and into acting. I made my professional debut in a short tour of the Whitehall farce, Simple Spymen, directed by Brian Rix (sort of nepotism twice removed) and worked for a year with Theatre Centre, based in Islington, doing shows in schools. At the same time I also moved back in with Helen and Jamie, who now had a flat in Clapham.

The three of us, under the name Murry Rix Wilton started sending scripts in for TV. Helen was working as a secretary at the BBC and was on 'Not the Nine o'clock News' at the time - we got two "quickies" on air. The next project was Three of a Kind, where we managed eventually to wangle a commission for 5 minutes of material a week. It was on this show that we met some other writers, Trevor McCallum, Kim Fuller and Vicki Pile; and together with them and the musician, Steve Brown (who I worked with on Newsrevue at the Gate in Notting Hill) we formed a revue group, Writers Inc, which toured round London playing pub venues and community centres. In August 1982 we took the show to Edinburgh, where we won the Perrier award.

So, Trevor McCallum, who we met on 'Three of a Kind', and who was part of Writers Inc, ended up being script editor on Playaway (ah, at last, a mention of some Children's TV!), so we started writing stuff for it and I got myself 4 episodes in the last series. There was then a decision to replace Playaway with something more contemporary and Trevor came up with the idea of Fast Forward, which Jamie and I wrote for, and which I performed in for 3 series (19shows). In the meantime I had got myself onto 'Carrott's Lib' in October 1982 following our Perrier win in September, and at some point (although the exact chronology is slightly confused in the mists of alcohol... sorry- time, I auditioned for and landed myself the part of Tony Deal, the con man, on 'No.73'.

It was an amazing experience. We'd meet on Tuesday and the script was just a list of scenes, with a brief description of the action and a time. We'd then spend the week writing the scenes through improvisation. Sandi Toksvig was brilliant-gag after gag after gag - you couldn't stop her. I think we rehearsed in London then moved down to Southampton/Maidstone on Friday. We rehearsed all day Friday on set (not sure if we had cameras, but I think possibly not) and I think the call on Saturday morning was 6 or possibly even 5, when we'd run the whole show for cameras before going live at 9. Friday nights were the best of all, because they'd put us up in a hotel and very often the guests for the show would stay too. I can't believe how late we stayed up and how much was drunk considering how early we had to get up the next morning. I'm pretty certain there was at least one occasion when I only got a couple of hours sleep. But hey! I was young.

My best memories are Dexy's Midnight Runners doing "Come On Eileen" at the end of the programme in the cellar and playing on for about 10 minutes after we went off air - and hosting the Sandwich Quiz one week when Sandi was off (with a lot of Bruce Forsythisms). Did I mention that Kim Goody was lovely? Well, she was. I think I only did about 4-6 shows each series and there was a period when I alternated between doing Tony Deal one week and Mo the Crow on Saturday Superstore on the other side.

Martin and Hazel (Richard and Jeannie) at Number 71 were both lovely. There was something wonderfully old- fashioned about their characters. I had great fun doing one of the 'No. 73' films with them (written by Sandi Toksvig and Nick Symons) where. I played Tony Vaselino, a rival of Martin's for Hazel's affections. we filmed down at the Leas cliff Pavilion theatre in Folkestone and it was great fun. I was shown up to be a rotter and a cad in the end (which required huge acting skill on my part). I don't know who the neighbours were on the other side. Maybe I wasn't paying attention.

It was great fun working in children's TV back in the 80's at the BBC, when they had a huge wardrobe and full time Make-up departments. Doing a sketch show like Fast Forward was like playing with the biggest dressing-up box in the world. I remember we had rails and rails of costumes we could chose from, and they had books with moustaches and beards in. There were two types of studio days - audience ones, where we'd rehearse all day and then do a show in front of a live audience, playing in pre-recorded sketches and rehearse/record days, which were my favourite, where we'd spend the whole day doing sketches in different sets and costumes. I think we'd start at 10 through till lunch at 1.00 then back at 2.00 to get into costume to start at 2.30 though till 6.00, then back 7.00 for 7.30 through till 10. It always used to get manic around 9.45 trying to get the last sketches done because we'd have to finish dead on time. They were long days but great fun.

We'd occasionally get fits of the giggles when we saw some unintended double entendre or something like that and the producers would go mad trying to get us to finish the sketch. The angrier they got the harder it would be to stop "corpsing". My best memories of Fast Forward come from the first series working with Joanna Munro and Andy Secombe, who used to crease me up with sudden bits of extra business. I remember onetime Andy and I having a bottle of Cotes de Rhone (his favourite tipple) hidden in wardrobe on one of the evenings of rehearse/record, but perhaps I should say nothing more about that! There are some other stories I could tell but I'd better keep them to myself unless I've got a lawyer present!

The last children's series I did (apart from an episode of 'Nuzzle & Scratch' and 2 episodes of Scoop in this millennium) was 'Wysiwyg' in 1991. The premise of the series was that terrestrial TV station, ITV, was interrupted by transmissions from IGTV (Intergalactic Television) controlled by Mer-Dokk (MD). In the first episode the supposed ITV programme is a take on "Blockbusters" called Jokebusters.

A lot of people missed it though. It was meant for older kids 9+ but they put it out when they were still at school. Also the first episode, setting up the whole premise, went out when one of those English hopefuls, Jeremy Bates, was being knocked out of the 4th round at Wimbledon in 5 sets over on BBC One. I also really messed up by having a fight over the rights, which I won, but lost in the long term because it meant they never repeated the series.

Budgets were a lot tighter and even though we were working for Yorkshire TV, we had to hire the studio from them (so we ended doing most of the show on location and only used the studio for a couple of days) and the camera crew was a separate company (even though part of the same overall company) I remember it was hard to get costumes sorted and we had problems with the camera one day and there wasn't the technical back up that here used to be - they had a real struggle getting a replacement out to us. Having said that the team was terrific and the props man Arthur Lake, the best in the business - really funny - very dry.

As for other work I spent a couple of months shut in a cupboard 'doing the bits between the programmes' for Children's ITV, and I particularly enjoyed playing "Noddy" (on a drink-drive charge) opposite Lord Denning. After reading a story for 'Jackanory', I was invited back in 1991 to write and read my own story, 'Fish Tale', for their 25th birthday celebrations, 'Silver Jackanory'. I also appeared in the four improvised Jackanory programmes, 'Pass the Story' and I was the voice in 'Going Live' where I 'did' the prizes for 'Double Dare'.

My recent experiences in 'Nuzzle & Scratch' and 'Scoop' have been good but the whole budget thing is much more obvious than it was back in the 80's. Not surprising I suppose. And casting's at much shorter notice (though that's true of all TV and theatre now i think) Filming's a lot quicker nowadays because it's so much easier working with smaller cameras, remote monitors etc.

When I was a child 'Crackerjack' was one of my favourite shows – with Lesley Crowther and Peter Glaze. I loved their routines when Glaze would demonstrate something to Crowther, who'd get it all wrong. Best of all was Peter Glaze's

Nick Wilton

growing frustration, always very physical, and his mastery of his own very special version of a double take, which somehow seemed to involve every muscle in his body. I do my own humble tribute to his genius most years in panto in scenes like the one in which Dame Trott tries to milk Daisy with help (or rather hinderance) from Silly Billy. Well, it makes me laugh.

I also liked the bit where Mr Derek tried to tell a story in the Basil Brush show, with Basil's constant interruptions plus the seemingly effortless banter between Morecambe and Wise as well as Tony Hancock, the Goons and Al Read on the radio at Sunday lunch time. I also enjoyed the cartoon inspired lunacy of 'The Goodies', listening to comedy records by the likes of The Smothers Brothers, Peter Sellers and Stan Freberg. Oh, and the children's TV series "Do Not Adjust Your Set".

The highlights of my career so far are definitely the thrill of working on live shows - 'Carrott's Lib', 'No. 73' and 'Saturday Superstore'. My favourite of all being the three series and specials of 'In One Ear' on BBC Radio 4, which I created with Jamie Rix. The failure of the TV version, 'Hello Mum', was one of my biggest disappointments - although I still maintain there was some really good stuff in there too.

Nick Wilton

For all the latest Nick Wilton news go to www.nickwilton.co.uk or visit his panto blog www.nickwiltonpanto.blogspot.co.uk

HENRY WOOLF
WORDS & PICTURES

Henry Woolf is another of these amazing people who I have to thank for helping to educate and entertain me as a child, alongside the uniquely animated Charlie and a magic pencil! A heavyweight of the theatre world, Henry had already been head of the East End mafia in Steptoe and Son and appeared as a partying Transylvanian in the cult film The Rocky Horror Show before opening the doors to his book shop.

Words and Pictures just fell into my lap. I had one meeting with the producer Moira Gambleton and that was that – the start of three happy years presenting the programme.

Henry Woolf

Moira was a very sensible, down to earth producer who didn't believe in talking down to children. I sometimes squirm at the false, enormous smiles and fake bon homie on some of today's childrens' programmes. Children can't be fooled for very long.

Charlie, or rather his manipulator, was a very original fellow. We got on very well but sometimes it felt very odd to be talking to an empty space on camera as Charlie was often dubbed in later in the editor's lab.

As an actor I've played a number of different characters. Frankie Barrow (in Steptoe & Son) was huge fun to play. Even now taxi drivers in London say to me "You were really evil as Frankie Barrow – really!!" and give me a doubtful look! My favourite moment was in the TV episode when the Kung Fu pensioner pinned me to the wall with a two pronged hay fork round my neck, very fast. Scary! No it wasn't. They shot it backwards of course.

Playing goodies and baddies is all one to me, but every actor I know prefers playing baddies and, on reflection, so do I.

I enjoyed doing the Time Warp very much. What a good movie 'Rocky Horror' is, but does anyone know that the unsung hero of the movie is an extra who stepped forward and caught Meatloaf in mid air as his Harley careered off the circular ramp saving him serious injury and snapping his own ankle in the process? No one ever thanked him, I believe.

There have been all kinds of different highlights in my career, for example, playing in Peter Brook's amazing production of 'Marat/Sade'; recently grappling with Samuel Beckett's Vladimir in 'Waiting for Godot' and directing the first production of Harold Pinter's first play 'The Room' way back in 1957."

Charlie

FRANCIS WRIGHT

DIBS (YOU AND ME), ART ATTACK, MOTORMOUTH, GROTBAGS, MORTIMER AND ARABEL, SWEEP (SOOTY SHOW)

Francis is definitely the man to go to if you want to know how to get 'a head' in puppetry! Literally, if you were a fan of Art Attack, but before those 'heady' days he was also one half of the iconic You & Me duo Cosmo and Dibs (he was the yellow one) along with a host of other TV programmes and classic children's dramas, not forgetting one famous squeaking pup.

I was born in St. John's Wood in a private nursing home, and the family house was in Crescent Grove, SW4 – a battered crescent of handsome late Georgian houses built for the ladies-in-waiting of Queen Charlotte, as far as I recall.

We left Crescent Grove in 1963 – just after I started school – and moved to Station Road, Barnes, SW13, where we stayed for 20 years. My first school was Glengyle Preparatory School for Boys in Carlton Drive, Putney, SW15.

At the age of 9, I was sent to Colet Court (St Paul's Preparatory School), which was at that time (1967) still housed in handsome Victorian red-brick buildings in Hammersmith – Colet Court on one side of the road, and St Paul's on the other, brooding at the end of its driveway.

Colet Court was an interesting and largely enjoyable experience, thanks in the main to one of the form masters, the always bright and good-humoured Alan Bateman (his initials 'AJSB' graced many an exercise book.) This lively and stylish young man had the knack of inspiring creativity, and I don't think any of us have ever forgotten him. As a class, we were very sorry when he left to take up a post in Canada, but the Canadians will have benefited enormously. He now lives and works in Kenya, where he has been a headmaster for many years.

Mr Bateman – always known affectionately as 'Batman' – was often responsible for 'The Colet Court Play' – an annual event which I was desperate to be part of. I was eventually cast as Little Buttercup in H.M.S. Pinafore –which suited my hystrionic tendencies, but probably did nothing to further the reputation of Coletine drama. The performance still exists on an LP – somewhere. Probably very scratched, and virtually unplayable. Just as well.

After leaving the senior school, St. Paul's, I studied drama, and graduated with honours. I decided to specialise in puppetry, which seemed to be a good way of never being typecast and/or doomed to a life mainly out of work.

My professional writing credits began with the BBC's long-running series 'Morning Story' – only 15 minutes of fame, but it was a start.

The first four years of my performing career were spent with a touring children's theatre company, the excellent Playboard Puppets, playing everything from a tortoise to a granny. Going 'freelance' then meant a year out of work – during which time I made ends meet by being a journalist, writing about British TV programmes and their stars for several European and worldwide publications.

I then became one of the two leading characters in a series for BBC Schools called 'You and Me' … My character's name was Dibs – or the yellow one, as he was known to those who could never remember the names. The rather downtrodden Dibs, and his opposite number, the gruff-voiced Cosmo (played by Frances Kay), carried on exploring life's little ups and downs for eleven years. They were created by producer Richard Callanan and made by Muppet maker and performer Tim Rose, and the scripts were written by members of the production team and cast. They were on the screen for pre-school kids from 1981 until 1992.

Dibs in fancy dress

Inspired by the direct and down-to-earth approach of 'Sesame Street', each programme featured a four-minute sketch on just about anything that a child might identify with: sharing, eating, arguing, bullying, sleeping, dressing up, being silly, having a row, make-believe, making poetry – the sky was the limit, as long as the sketch was relevant and useful to the target audience.

The scripts didn't patronise: they informed, educated, and entertained – and the high quality of the writing deliberately saw the world from a child's point of view. A successful group of sketches dealing with 'Safety' included the tricky subject of child abuse – making 'You and Me' something of a trail-blazer. It was welcomed by the charity, Kidscape, and featured on the national news.

Songs and stories were always included, with an emphasis on cultural diversity – 'You and Me' was one of the few programmes of the time to do this.

The enthusiastic production team was committed to the ethos of the programme in its new form. In previous years, 'You and Me' had been fronted by characters such as Crow and Alice, Mr Bits-and-Pieces, Duncan the Dragon, and Herbert the Handyman.

The advent of Cosmo and Dibs took away the safely middle-class element of the show, introducing a rougher edge – an edge reflecting the world that a modern child might experience every day.

Documentary features brought along a wealth of subjects ranging from the colour and exuberance of the Notting Hill Carnival to the mud and hard graft of farming. Henry the Kangaroo – with his catchphrase 'I'm looking for the words in my book again' – introduced simple social sight words (Stop, Go, Bus, Train, Station, etc.) to Ellie and her Dad and the audience. Cartoon Henry was animated by Mike Hibbert, and voiced by Nigel Lambert.

The theme music was also given a facelift. Gone was the jangling that had always accompanied an array of animated building blocks. Instead, viewers were treated to a line of children (again animated by Mike Hibbert) dancing to a reggae version of the title song, re-recorded by UB40.

Now, the programme featured human presenters that were a cross-section of ethnic backgrounds. Among them were Jeni Barnett, Charubala Chokshi, Harry Towb, Larrington Walker, Liz Smith, Gary Wilmot, Annette Badland, Sheila Chitnis, Mike Grady, Isabelle Lucas, Michael Snelders, Maggie Ollerenshaw, Bharti Patel, Indira Joshi, Yasmin Pettigrew and Bill Owen. Clive Mason also joined the cast for programmes relevant to the deaf community.

The set, based on a street market in London's Shepherd's Bush, evolved steadily over the years under different designers: Mark Savant, Rosemary Hester, David Bevin and Rory Mitchell were among those who brought the market stalls to life.

The first series of twenty programmes was begun at the BBC's Lime Grove Studios, part of which overlooked Shepherd's Bush Market. It was completed at BBC Television Centre in Wood Lane, which became the show's regular home for all but the last series.

Changing times and changing trends dictated that 'You and Me' too would change. A sour letter from a school intimated that 'our kids need therapy to turn on the telly' – and suddenly everything had to be more 'fun!' Additional puppet characters joined Cosmo and Dibs for the last two seasons, and the street market disappeared in favour of a brightly-coloured domestic setting.

In 1992, an independent production company took the helm, and at the dawning of the Age of Teletubbies an element of middle-class cosiness was brought back to the programme for its final airing.

My other credits include the Psammead in the BBC's teatime classic children's drama 'Five Children and It', the Phoenix in 'The Phoenix and the Carpet', the

Francis and producer Nic Ayling with 'The Head' from Art Attack

evil Sybil Sludge in 'The Spooks of Bottle Bay', and the March Hare in Hallmark Films' version of 'Alice in Wonderland', which boasted a cast more star-studded than the Milky Way.

I featured as 'The Head' in ITV'S 'Art Attack' and 'Art Attack International' for many years, and also co-wrote and performed three series (78 half-hours) of 'Bug Alert!' for Channel 4 and ITV. I even became an icon of sorts when I inherited the role of Sweep in 'Sooty'. This involved having to squeak a lot, and frequently get covered in custard.

Other series included 'Panic Station', 'Spitting Image', 'Motormouth', 'Grotbags', Mortimer and Arabel', 'Jay's World', 'Beachcomber Bay', 'Gophers!', and many more over 20 years.

I also teach personal presentation and speaking skills – for anyone who wants to develop the way they come across in public. Clients could be performers, business executives, interview candidates who need a confidence-booster – or dad who has to speak at his daughter's wedding.

After lecturing on communication to the Business Studies students at Middlesex University, I was asked to take part in the Reality Show 'American Princess' for

Francis (Dibs) and Frances Kay (Cosmo)

Granada/NBC, which involved helping to turn ten American girls from all walks of life into young ladies.

Recent projects include narrating two 10-part series: 'B&B The Best' (for BBC TV), followed by 'Rosemary Shrager's Kitchen Showdown' (for ITV Daytime), and appearing on 'The Paul O'Grady Show' – teaching Paul to 'speak proper'!

I also appeared as Thomas Becket in TS Eliot's 'Murder in the Cathedral'. The production celebrated the 75th anniversary of the play's premiere, and was – like the 1935 original – mounted by Radius (The Religious Drama Society of Great Britain.) It was staged in the tiny 13th century Sussex church of St Mary, North Stoke, and was directed by Brian E. Cook. The following year, I was asked to take part in a performance of readings celebrating the 400th anniversary of the King James Bible, and recently played a variety of roles in 'Shakespeare Soup' – a revue about the Bard and all his works.

Francis Wright

To peruse Francis' weblog and to see more photos from many of the programmes mentioned please visit www.franciswright.wordpress.com

 # IN MEMORIAM

Many extremely creative and talented people who have been instrumental in our upbringing and entertainment are, sadly, no longer with us. Please take a moment to remember those who have given so much.

BOB BLOCK - Rentaghost

RICHARD CARPENTER - Catweazle, The Boy From Space

CLIVE DUNN - Grandad

MARK HALL - Cosgrove Hall

BOB HOLNESS - Blockbusters

JOE LYNCH - Chorlton and the Wheelies

JERRY NELSON - The Count (Sesame Street), The Muppets, Fraggle Rock

CHRIS SIEVEY - Frank Sidebottom

ERIC THOMPSON - The Magic Roundabout

GEORGE WOODBRIDGE - (Inigo Pipkin - Pipkins)

MURIEL YOUNG (Auntie Mu) - A Handful of Songs

TERRY NUTKINS - Animal Magic, The Really Wild Show

I would just like to say a few words about Terry who passed away this year (2012). I'd been in touch with him and we'd spoken briefly about this book and he was keen to be part of it, but sadly he was taken from us before our chat could take place. It was as an enormous shock for everyone. His love for animals and wildlife was unmistakable and I'm sure they felt his loss just as much as we did. - Garry Vaux

Bye Bye

Everybody

Bye Bye